AN INTROD
ELIJAH MUHA

The New Educational Paradigm

Abul Pitre

Elijah Muhammad Studies:
Interdisciplinary, Educational, and Islamic Studies Series

University Press of America,® Inc.
Lanham · Boulder · New York · Toronto · Plymouth, UK

**Copyright © 2010 by
University Press of America,® Inc.**
4501 Forbes Boulevard
Suite 200
Lanham, Maryland 20706
UPA Acquisitions Department (301) 459-3366

Estover Road
Plymouth PL6 7PY
United Kingdom

Library of Congress Control Number: 2009931980
ISBN: 978-0-7618-4780-9 (paperback : alk. paper)
eISBN: 978-0-7618-4781-6

Dedicated to my grandmother (Mother)
who has shaped me for THEM.

Contents

Series Foreword

Elijah Muhammad Studies: An Interdisciplinary, Educational, and Islamic Studies Series

Elijah Muhammad Studies represents the beginning of the new educational paradigm. Minister Farrakhan in his newly released study guide titled, *The Education Challenge: A New Educational Paradigm for the 21st Century,* lays the foundation for deeper study into the field of education and its significance in bringing to birth the educational paradigm shift that will produce a New World. He writes, "This is telling us the type of thing we are and must be engaged in, which is to stimulate or challenge our intellect over the problem that is found in education" (Farrakhan, 2009, p. 11). A paradigm shift in education is indeed a daunting and challenging task. The task of shifting the paradigm in education is problematic because of the historical structuring that has fueled the cultural experiences of the masses who live within worlds and systems that are tied to the educational system. If we define education as "leading out" or "bringing forth" the attributes that are within the human being for the greater good of the system or organization, then education has served the interest of the powerful. Dr. Muhammad Yunus gives an example of the impact of systems on the development of culture, attitudes, and dispositions when he describes the current capitalist system as striving on the idea of profit. Yunus (2007) argues that profit caters to the more selfish characteristics of the individual, thus systems under this kind of thinking do not bring forth the totality of human goodness. He proposes that we look at new systems, one of which he refers to as social business. Opposed to building organizations that build on the profit motive he proposes a system that is philosophically developed on giving (social business)—which brings forth another dimension of the human being—creating a different world. A world that answers in the affirmative to the question posed to Jesus: When were you hungry and we fed you not? When were you thirsty and we didn't give you drink? The system proposed by Yunus seems to address the *least of these.* It is a system that undermines the current educational and organizational systems that work in the interest of producing "things," not authentic human beings (Freire, 2000).

At the core of the educational system in America is the corporate capitalist interest in getting an ample supply of workers whose labor can be used in the interest of the ruling elite. The corporate capitalist interest in education has resulted in an educational system that is developed along tiers. These tiers situate the roles that individuals will play within the system (Bowles cited in Noel, 2008). A small elite group of students will receive an education that will make them leaders and producers, while the masses of students will receive an education that makes them followers and consumers. Jean Anyon (1981) describes the differing schools in an article titled, *Social Class and the Hidden Curriculum of Work*. In this article, she identifies four different schools—*working class schools, middle class schools, affluent schools,* and *executive elite schools.* In these schools, the curriculum reflected the future roles that students were expected to assume once they completed their education. Farrakhan (2009) summarizes, "You have an educational system that has an elite at the top, then a lesser elite and a lesser elite, then the mass who work for the elite" (p. 17). This type of education—one to produce workers for corporate capitalist interest—has been called by some mis-education (Chomsky, 2000; Woodson, 1999).

America's educational systems, like all systems, are rooted in rules of discourse, language, artifacts, symbols, etc., that are imbedded into disciplines or fields of studies. These fields or disciplines are grounded in theoretical constructs that are largely driven by European conceptions of these fields. For example in the field of education John Dewey is considered a major philosophical figure. Dewey's brilliance of ideas, while rightfully studied, takes on a form of divinity as his ideas become the foundation for the philosophical discourse in education. The field of education like other fields or disciplines is dominated by European males who have shaped the discourse and language of the field. While Dewey is mentioned in schools of education, Carter G. Woodson is absent from the discourse in most schools of education that prepare students. In a doctoral-level education course, I asked some students if they had ever heard of Carter G. Woodson. To my surprise most students responded they had never heard of him. This is an example of the problematic nature of shifting paradigms. The rules, language, symbols, artifacts, and discourse have been built by Europeans. This is a form of White supremacy that is invisible. So invisible that it gives the impression that education is neutral and does not have political implications. It also gives birth to hegemony—consent by the oppressed to be dominated by those who rule. Individuals who question the prevailing order of education would be looked upon as disrupting the good system that will help children get a job. The current educational system prepares educators to view the problem of education and society from the mind of the ruling elite, thus giving them a view of the oppressed "as marginal persons who deviate from the general configuration of a 'good, organized, and just' society" (Freire, 2000, p. 24). Watkins (2001a) illuminates this idea when he says, "Organized education, much like organized religion, has long been influenced by the forces of the power structure, the state, and those with an ideological agenda" (p. 10). Educators educated under such a system in turn become oppressors because, "The White man is the god of his own world, and his idea is to make everybody into his own image and after his own likeness" (Farrakhan, 2009, p. 27). The White man refers to the embodiment of an idea or way of viewing the world that is alien to the aboriginal people. It then becomes a necessity to create a new paradigm. Let us turn to examining the questions: what is a paradigm?

Thomas Kuhn (1962) is credited with shaping the contemporary terminology identified as a paradigm. Kuhn's work has been specifically related to the field of science with a focus on the history of science. His definition of a paradigm centered on how an experiment would be conducted and what equipment would be used to conduct the experiment. Depending on how one defines science, this could apply to the mastery of an area of study or perhaps higher degrees of knowledge within a field or discipline. Handa (1986) advanced Kuhn's ideas about a paradigm to include the social sciences and the field of education. A paradigm in the social sciences and education would refer to the way one sees or views the world. Banks (2008) defines a paradigm as, "An interrelated set of facts, concepts, generalizations, and theories that attempt to explain human behavior or social phenomenon and that imply policy and action" (p. 135). In sum, a paradigm is a cognitive view of the world that is shaped by ideas imbedded in institutions. At the foundation of shaping ideas are the educational systems which give rise to how one views the world.

The challenge of shifting educational paradigms becomes very problematic because it disrupts the prevailing structure of the entire world order. Pinar et.al, (2008) cogently argues, "When a field shifts from one major paradigm to another, many scholars are left with allegiances to concepts that are no longer pertinent" (p. 13). This is equivalent to replacing one god with a new god. If we take the definition of God as being the supreme in knowledge, wisdom, and understanding, then those who hold the powerful positions in the society have been able to rule as gods of the present world. A major reason they have been able to rule is because they have "carefully selected and sponsored knowledge, which contributed to obedience, subservience, and docility" (Watkins, 2001b, p.39). Once a greater and more powerful being emerges, he becomes the God of the New World. Prior to this emergence the two Gods are locked in a secret battle regarding whose knowledge or ideas will rule into the future. The idea of the Supreme Being (God) is to destroy Satan and his world. The educational arena then becomes the key to freeing people from the grips of a satanic world.

Elijah Muhammad serves as a marker for the transition of worlds. Born in a country that had dehumanized Black people and reduced them to "beings for others," Muhammad was raised among the most rejected and despised people of America. His 1930 encounter with Wallace Fard Muhammad was the impetus for the educational paradigm shift that is now emerging in a universal way. The meeting between the two started a process of awakening people to a much bigger reality. That reality being: God is a man. When Elijah Muhammad began to disclose the historical, theological, scientific exegesis of the Universe and its origination, he shifted the entire educational paradigm. He declared that he met with God in person and was designated as the Messenger of God. This type of teaching was heretical and posed a great danger to his life. He was attacked for over forty years for teaching profound truths that destroyed the power of White supremacy. The entire mission of Elijah Muhammad was educational and this is clearly noticeable when he makes mention that his teacher studied every educational system in the civilized world. This is very significant because he does not say he studied every science or history book, but he studied every educational system. In modern terms, this is called comparative education.

Comparative education's historical development has been described as "the period of travelers tales" (Noah & Eckstein, 1998, p. 15). Kubow and Fossum (2007) note, "These comparative studies examined educational systems, specifically the structure, organization, and method of education in other countries. These visitors—educators and politicians—based their judgments on their own impressions of other cultures" (p. 8). This aligns perfectly with the experiences of Elijah Muhammad's teacher Master Fard Muhammad. According to Elijah Muhammad, his teacher visited every inhabited place on the earth—Master Fard Muhammad is a worldwide traveler. His international experiences and his teachings to Elijah Muhammad were preparation for the Universal education that he was preparing for the New World. Elijah Muhammad declared, "What Allah has revealed to me is a base for building universal knowledge. It has not become universal or we would not be preaching. It is to become universal" (Pitre, 2008). Could this universal knowledge be in some way related to teleology, the study of design and purpose of the Universe and man's role in that Universe? A deeper and more careful examination of the teachings of Elijah Muhammad reveals that his teachings contain universal knowledge. This universal knowledge is related to every field and discipline of study found in major research universities throughout the world. The educational paradigm shift is profound because the body of knowledge that has come into existence is emanating from another source, beyond the White supremacist educational structure. In the 1930's when Elijah Muhammad declared that there was life on Mars as well other planets this was shocking. Today we see a field of study called astrobiology—the study of life on other planets. Additionally, his message to the downtrodden Blacks of America was to get the knowledge of self. The knowledge of self forms the basis of elite education. What Elijah Muhammad brought was a Supreme Education that exceeded the gods (scientists, scholars) of this world. He writes, "However no education of this world of the white race will be accepted in the new world. For the new world you have a new education and government. The God of the New World is a New God" (Muhammad, 1974, p. 124). He goes on to say, "first He Makes a New Mind for us and a New Way of thinking. He teaches us a different education, one we never had before" (p. 123). This is the ultimate paradigm shift!

If we look at the current educational system, we see that it is a very powerful world. Close your eyes and envision the higher education institutions in America. Now think about the major research universities that you see competing every week on television during football and basketball season. The crowds for football games exceed 100,000 at several major research schools. Look into the crowds and you will notice that they are predominantly White. The institutions that are conducting ground-breaking research, dictating policy, shaping American and international life is taking place at these major White universities. The physical structures of these universities are replicas of cities within cities. Just being in the environment of these institutions creates a different mindset. The knowledge in these universities is the life blood for the larger society. So the reality is that the oppressed are dealing with a power that is unconquerable-without a greater degree of knowledge—because the knowledge in these institutions is in the domain of a majority White population situated in a White supremacist infrastructure. Tynnetta Muhammad explains, "Master Fard Muhammad comes up against all the educational systems of the old world order" (Pitre, 2008, p. xii). Ironically, Elijah Muhammad has penetrated the infrastructure of higher educational centers. This has created an unusual phenomena leading to the total collapse of the present world order which will give rise to the new.

Elijah Muhammad Studies: An Interdisciplinary, Educational, and Islamic Studies Series is designed to crack open the teachings of Elijah Muhammad to build a more universal knowledge that can free human beings from the current world order that deprives them from being Gods. The series, while centered on education, is interdisciplinary and also has a focus on Islamic studies. Islam in this sense is beyond common notions of religion but can be viewed as a universal way of life that governs all of creation. This approach allows for a dynamic study of every imaginable field with the possibility of creating new fields of study. The series is the first of its kind to examine the interdisciplinary, educational, and Islamic scope of Elijah Muhammad's work. In the past, scholars have drawn solely on historical developments and sociological studies of Elijah Muhammad, but have not examined the depth of his teaching as it relates to every discipline of study. This series examines the interdisciplinary scope of Elijah Muhammad's work across disciplines. Thus a wide range of scholars from diverse disciplines and fields will have an opportunity to submit scholarly academic work juxtaposing the teachings of Elijah Muhammad, within their respective areas of study.

Another component of the series will be the examination of Elijah Muhammad's teaching as it relates specifically to the field of education. The study of education is the core of the series, focusing on a wide range of topics within the field of education. Some of those topics include multicultural education, critical pedagogy, critical race theory, theology, white studies, curriculum theory, and educational leadership. Educational scholars will have the opportunity to submit book projects that address education in the 21st century.

The Islamic Studies aspect of the series will stimulate renewed discourse about Elijah Muhammad and the role he played in advancing Islam in America. There are several major universities in the U.S. that offer programs in Islamic Studies. The discourse in some of the Islamic Studies programs do not adequately address the impact of Elijah Muhammad and his role in laying a foundation for Islamic Studies in the U.S.; millions of dollars have been donated to major universities to develop programs and institutes, as well as centers in Islamic Studies. The post 9/11 world has created a growing interest in Islam; and according to Banks (2008), Islam is the fastest growing religion in the U.S., with the largest number of converts being African Americans. The series will be at the forefront of researching this new phenomena and the growing American interest in Islam as it relates to Elijah Muhammad.

An Introduction to Elijah Muhammad Studies: The New Educational Paradigm is the first book in the series. It attempts to offer a theoretical grounding for developing the field. The book, while heavily focused on education with a specific focus on Black education, is designed to extend the notion of Black as being universal. Elijah Muhammad specifically pointed out that some were calling him a Black nationalist; however he argued that Black was not national, it was universal. The ultimate goal of the book and series is to crack the teachings of Elijah Muhammad for the building of universal knowledge. Additionally, the book addresses the interdisciplinary scope of Elijah Muhammad's teachings which provides a way of juxtaposing the teachings with academic subjects.

An Introduction to Elijah Muhammad Studies: The New Educational Paradigm, as well as other books in the series, will be of interest to lay persons, scholars, students, and world leaders both nationally and internationally. The recent announcement of a *New Beginning* for the Nation of Islam has created discourse on the universality of Elijah Muhammad's work and what it means for all people regardless of race, class, or religion. The series is compelling and the first of its kind to potentially attract scholars nationally and internationally around the teachings of Elijah Muhammad.

Abul Pitre, Series Co-editor
Associate Professor
Educational Leadership
Fayetteville State University

References

Anyon, J. (1981). Social class and the hidden curriculum of work. *Curriculum Inquiry* 11, No. 81: 27.

Banks, J. (2008). *An introduction to multicultural education.* 4th ed. Boston, MA: Pearson Education.

Chomsky, N. (2000). Chomsky on mis-education. Lanham, MD. Rowman and Littlefield.

Farrakhan, L. (2009). *The education challenge: A new educational paradigm for the 21st Century.* Chicago, IL: Final Call.

Freire, P. (2000). *Pedagogy of the oppressed.* New York, NY: Continuum.

Handa, M. L. (1986) *Peace paradigm: Transcending liberal and Marxian paradigms.* Paper presented in International Symposium on Science, Technology and Development. New Delhi, India.

Kubow, P. & Fossum, P. (2006). *Comparative education: Exploring issue in international context* (2nd ed.). Upper Saddle River, NJ: Pearson.

Kuhn, T.S. (1962). *The structure of scientific revolutions.* Chicago: University of Chicago Press.

Muhammad, E. (1974). *Our savior has arrived.* Chicago, IL: Final Call.

Noah, J. & Eckstein, M.A. (1998). *Doing comparative education: Three decades of collaboration.* Hong Kong: Comparative Education Research Centre.

Noel, J. (2008). *Notable selections in multicultural education.* 2nd ed. New York: McGraw Hill.

Pinar, W., Reynolds, W., Slattery, P., & Tubman, P. (2008). *Understanding curriculum.* New York: Peter Lang.

Pitre, A. (2008). *The educational philosophy of Elijah Muhammad. Education for a new world.* 2nd ed. Lanham, MD: University Press of America.

Watkins, W. (2001a). *The White architects of Black education: Ideology and power in America 1865–1954.* New York: Teachers College Press.

————. (2001b). Blacks and the curriculum: From accommodation to contestation and beyond. In Watkins, W., Lewis, J. & Chou, V. *Race and education: The roles of history and society in educating African American students (p*p. 40-66). Needham Heights, MA: Allyn and Bacon.

Woodson, C. G. (1999). *The mis-education of the Negro.* 11th ed. Trenton, NJ: First Africa World Press.

Yunus, M. (2007). *Creating a world without poverty: Social business and the future of capitalism.* New York: Public Affairs.

Preface

The global economic crisis and its impact on the world's institutions are creating panic among the citizens of the U.S. and the world. Educational institutions across the U.S. are being asked to trim their budgets, forcing nearly every educational institution to contend with doing more while having fewer resources. Clearly, the economic crisis is bringing about change. These monumental changes were not the change that the masses were anticipating.

Elijah Muhammad, in his forty-four years of teaching in America, warned that a time was coming in America where her financial security would be weakened. He spoke clearly about the collapse of the dollar and the eventual collapse of the American government. In his book, *The Fall of America*, he devoted an entire chapter to the Fall of America's Educational System. The changes that Elijah Muhammad foresaw ultimately included a complete educational paradigm shift. The paradigm shift in education would give rise to a New World.

Today we are experiencing all of the events that Elijah Muhammad disclosed in the 1930s. The vast majority of social science work on Elijah Muhammad has not scratched the surface of what he really taught, leaving the masses with a limited view of this Master Teacher. In schools of education, colleges, and universities, Elijah Muhammad has been nameless despite the fact that many of the ground-breaking discoveries in academia have bases in what he taught.

In this ground-breaking work, *An Introduction to Elijah Muhammad Studies: The New Educational Paradigm*, the reader is given a sneak preview of the teachings of Elijah Muhammad and its multifaceted interdisciplinary scope. The book attempts to lay a foundation for situating the teachings of Elijah Muhammad in academia, creating a field of study that particularly extrapolates the jewels of Muhammad's teachings.

There is no doubt that a careful study of Elijah Muhammad's teachings will translate into real change—change we can really believe in!

Abul Pitre
April 2009
Fayetteville, NC

Acknowledgments

I am indeed thankful for my first student Leroy Simien, who was considered a problem student at the high school where I taught, for introducing me to Elijah Muhammad's book, *Message to the Black Man in America.* I thank this student for planting a seed that would grow into a much deeper understanding and love for Elijah Muhammad's work. A great depth of gratitude is in order for Minister Harold Muhammad, who started the fire for understanding Elijah Muhammad. I am also appreciative of Minister Lyle, the former Lafayette, Louisiana, study group leader, who kept the fire going and answered questions when I needed answers to understanding Elijah Muhammad. To my spiritual brother Gary, who has watched me labor in this work and offered words of encouragement every day. I am grateful! I am also thankful for my friend and big brother, Dr. Abdulalim Shabazz, for being a reflection of his teacher Elijah Muhammad. I have never met a scholar who has remained humbled and committed to the education of Black youth. I am eternally grateful that our paths have crossed. Dr. Shabazz is indeed the unconquerable one. Sister Dr. Dorothy Fardan deserves thanks for being such a beautiful sister. Dr. Fardan read through the first draft and suggested that I move forward immediately with publication of the book. A special thanks to Sister Lydia who has been supportive of this work, providing correspondence with The National House. To my brother Farrakhan, thanks for letting me get into your mind and sharing your insights about Elijah Muhammad. It is because of you that he lives in many. I am always and forever indebted to my brother and Pastor Dale Fontenot. Thanks for giving me a universal understanding and for being The Good Shepherd who has fed me when I was hungry and counseled me when I saw the face of death. Finally, to my wife Ruby, for being able to deal with the time and emotions of writing a book; thanks for your patience. To my daughters Ajah and Alaiah, you are gifts from God that I cherish each and every day. To my newborn son Alijah (baby man), I see the powerful handiwork of God in you each day. To my parents (Donald and Mamie) I thank you for preparing me for my life's mission— a servant.

Introduction

We are living in an exciting time in world history. In fact, this is a very momentous time to be alive—witnessing the explosion of knowledge. The knowledge explosion has encompassed every field and discipline of study. Scholars in the field of education are conceptualizing new approaches in the education of the human being. At the heart of these new approaches to education have been curriculum theorists and educational leadership scholars who are having conversations about the post-modern world. Post-modern ideas are beginning to make headway in the education field. The post-modern has been described as something like a bridge between the old and the new. The scholars of post-modernism assert that we have now entered into a new world that has surpassed the modern. Doll (1993) has described the phenomenon as the new science which is conceptualizing new ways of understanding curriculum theory. He notes that, in the new science, the post-modern era curriculum should not be viewed as a closed system but rather an open system. Cosmology, hermeneutics, and theology are being revisited in the post-modern. For curriculum theorists this moment represents what might be considered a revolution. A revolution, not in the sense that it is being fought with weapons, but a revolution that entails conceptualizing new ways of bringing forth the god potential in the human being by constructing curricula that brings forth creative powers. This new way of conceptualizing education has created culture wars whereby things that were once considered "truth" are being challenged. Post-modern thinking is disrupting much of the White supremacist logic that has enslaved the masses. Thus the post-modern scholars find themselves in a battle to free the mind. Despite the headway that post-modern thought is having with regard to disrupting White supremacist logic, there are others who see it still lacking with regard to issues of race and racism.

Part of the reason for such sentiment may be a result of what Doll describes in his text, *A Post-Modern Perspective on Curriculum Theory*. In his book, Doll specifically addresses issues related to concepts found in what is called the new science. Post-modern scholarship has fueled questions with regard to the universe and its origins. Doll (1993) notes, "Even in the sciences, a newness is emerging . . . Today, in the last decade of this century and millennium, we are in the midst of forming a new paradigm" (p.2). The new science—with connections to cosmology, hermeneutics, and theology—if carefully juxtaposed with teaching of Elijah Muhammad, opens an array of conversations related race and racism. Elijah Muhammad addressed each of the aforementioned strands with more depth analysis than scholars in the post-modern. Recently Minister Farrakhan (2008a), a student of Elijah Muhammad, delivered a lecture that specifically challenged educators to create a new educational paradigm. The lecture covered hermeneutics, theology, and the new world. There are clear linkages between

Doll's post modern work and the teachings of Elijah Muhammad (Doll, 1993; Muhammad 1965, 1973, 1974).

While Elijah Muhammad is not mentioned by post-modern scholars, the origin of post-modernism may have gleaned deeper insights from the little Black man born in rural Georgia. Elijah Muhammad did not use the term post-modern—a term used by scholars to confuse the masses—he simply described post-modern as the New World. However, unlike the scholars who base much of their work in theoretical constructs, Elijah Muhammad's exegesis of the New World was divine revelation. He gave a profound view of what the New World would look like. In his book, *Our Savior Has Arrived*, in the chapter titled: *He Makes All Things New*, he profoundly discloses elements of the New World. Any scholar who has read this work is immediately moved to begin thinking new thoughts. I contend that those in high places have taken this knowledge and used it to form ideas about a New World. In his exegesis of the New World one can gain access into what education and curriculum would encompass in the New World. Muhammad (1974) articulates, "He teaches us a different education, one we never had before. He gives us education on the wisdom, knowledge, understanding of Gods . . . not of prophets . . . but of the Gods of the prophets past" (p.123). He disclosed that there was an entirely new teaching that would emerge and form the basis of the new world: "We have to have new teachings." In the new world education would be designed to bring forth the God essence in the human being. The new knowledge would coincide with a new universe—cosmology—a new way of life that would be hand-delivered by God in person, thus setting a new course for understanding the God power within the human being—a new theology. Muhammad, unlike the scholars in the post-modern, was not theorizing about the new world but he had an accurate picture of what the new world would look like.

The post-modern scholars have set the stage for the emergence of *Elijah Muhammad Studies*. In arguing that hermeneutics is central to understanding education and curriculum building, post-modern scholars have expanded the discourse in education. These scholars note that hermeneutics is an interpretation of scripture. They brilliantly enunciate the Greek origin of hermeneutics referring to Hermes, who is considered the messenger of God responsible for relaying the messages of the Gods to the people in a language that they could understand. Slattery (2006) notes that, "The Greek hermeneuein ("to interpret") referred to Hermes, the winged messenger of the Greek gods, who explained the decisions of the gods to other gods and to mortal humans" (p. 130). Doll (2003) adds, "As the messenger-god, Hermes not only had to deliver messages from the gods to humans; he also had to interpret these messages into a form 'human intelligence could grasp' " (p. 135). This simple etymological explanation of hermeneutics opens the door for a much deeper conversation about the identity of Elijah Muhammad. Elijah Muhammad is most widely known as the Messenger of God. The knowledge he brings reveals the identity of God which had not been known for over 76 trillion years—since the beginning of creation. In the widely read book, *Message to the Black Man in America*, he opens by asking the question: Who is God? He addresses questions, like why are we using the term God. Elijah Muhammad interpreted the scriptures in a way that has reshaped all fields and disciplines of study. When he was physically or openly present among the people, he demonstrated beyond a doubt that he was indeed taught by a supreme teacher. Like Hermes he made the message or interpretation of the scriptures easy to understand. In fact, his work among the unlearned of the society demonstrates the simplicity and yet the complexity of his teachings. His teachings were easy to grasp for the masses but baffling to the rulers who could not understand how this man not having letters was learned beyond the scope of their civilization. However, unlike Hermes, Elijah Muhammad was not a trickster though some have tried to align him in this manner. The misrepresentations, the gross misunderstandings of what he taught have resulted in many of the scholars overlooking his work and its implications for the New World.

The scholars on post-modern education have done a tremendous job in preparing or setting the stage for an introduction to *Elijah Muhammad Studies*. Post-modern scholars have actually brought to the forefront an opportunity to revisit the teachings of Elijah Muhammad.

As a result of this I have taken the opportunity to introduce a new field of study called *Elijah Muhammad Studies*. This work is an introductory work into the academic study of the teachings of Elijah Muhammad, the interdisciplinary-universal scope of what Elijah Muhammad taught. Elijah Muhammad, in describing the modern and post modern world, retorted that our modern world is kindergarten knowledge for the original man, implying that all these modern advances were of no comparison to what lay in store in the New World. *Elijah Muhammad Studies* attempts to set the stage for a wide range of scholarly research related to the teachings of Elijah Muhammad.

Clearly, the teachings of Elijah Muhammad are already taking place in every major university in the world. The scholars do not openly proclaim that they are studying what Elijah Muhammad taught; however, if you carefully examine the greatest discoveries in all fields of knowledge you will find questions, ideas, exegetes of the teachings of Elijah Muhammad. *An Introduction to Elijah Muhammad Studies* allows the scholars in every field and discipline of study to look at the origins of what they are studying in relationship to what Elijah Muhammad taught. *An Introduction to Elijah Muhammad Studies: The New Educational Paradigm* is an introductory work that promises to be an eternal journey in the quest to ascertain the God knowledge.

Book Overview

An Introduction to Elijah Muhammad Studies is designed to create a much deeper examination of the teachings of Elijah Muhammad. This field of study is specifically designed to examine the universal aspect of his teachings. While some correctly assume that universal applies to the diversity of peoples and cultures, another dimension of the universal aspect of Elijah Muhammad teachings deals with his teachings about the universe. Elijah Muhammad specifically pointed out that the Muhammad University of Islam teaches the universe. Additionally, he declared that he was taught something about everything that existed in the universe. Jabril Muhammad writes that Elijah Muhammad talked about an experience where he was able to see the mind of God in creating the universe. Recently, Minister Farrakhan (2008b) one of the most noted contemporary students of Elijah Muhammad opened the mosque to all people, religious groups, etc. His lecture *A New Beginning* was very profound, laying a base for universal understanding of Elijah Muhammad's mission. Ironically, at major universities across the United States centers have emerged that are devoted to the study of Islam. One such center is at Duke University where there is a center for the study of Islam. Duke University's Islamic Study Center houses a rare copy of an Ethiopian Holy Quran. The study of Islam is now spreading in academic institutions in the U.S., paving the way for a much deeper understanding of Elijah Muhammad. Several scholars have expressed that Elijah Muhammad is responsible for laying the foundation for Islam in the United States.

Since its inception in the 1930s the Nation of Islam has weathered persecution in a country that claims to be founded on the principles of freedom, justice, and equality—with religious freedom being a major component. The history of the Nation of Islam in America unfortunately has been one of constant persecution. Despite the good works in promoting education, health care, jobs, decency, respect of people, and a commitment to the principles of freedom, justice, and equality for oppressed peoples, it has been demonized by the ruling powers. This has resulted in media coverage that has distorted the Nation of Islam making it appear as a religion of fanatic terrorists, hate teachings, and heathenism. The Nation of Islam has had to deal with government agents who have been placed within its apparatus with the hopes of destroying it. This along with concocted myths have limited the illuminating spirituality of Islam and its beauty to bring one into the crystallization with the teachings of Christ that would give its adherents supernatural powers. Imam Warith Deen Muhammad son of Elijah Muhammad once said that he did not have any education degrees but he had Islam which was something very powerful in the way of education. Elijah Muhammad clearly laid the foundation for Islam in America. Thus, universities across the country would be well served to implement *Elijah Muhammad Studies* independently, as a part of Islamic study centers, or as a component of Black Studies. The dilemma has been that most of the Islamic centers have been sponsored by Kings from various Middle Eastern countries, making them have a focus that is entirely on Middle Eastern cultural aspects of Islam. Some of these Kings have contributed millions of dollars to major academic institutions for the study of Islam. This has led to the absence of the most historical Islamic figure in American history: Elijah Muhammad. Berg (2009) in his newly released book *Elijah Muhammad and Islam,* similarly writes, "Its leader for almost forty years, Elijah Muhammad was therefore arguably the most important person in the development of Islam in America . . ." (p. 2). Even more disheartening is that the majority of Islamic Studies programs are housed in predominately White institutions. Historically, Black Colleges and Universities are absent when it comes to one of the most important of academic subjects. The idea of presenting *Elijah Muhammad Studies* as a field is that it will give scholars and laypersons new understanding of the teachings of Elijah Muhammad.

The time demands that we rethink Elijah Muhammad! The little man that the builders rejected needs to be understood, thus the scholars of Islam, Christianity, Judaism, and other faiths would be well served by digging much deeper into the depth of his teachings. *An Introduction to Elijah Muhammad Studies* attempts to create a new scholarly analysis of the teachings of Elijah Muhammad. The book has four chapters that are devoted to providing some insight into the universality of Muhammad's teachings. Chapter 1 is an introduction to the field *Elijah Muhammad Studies*. The chapter lays a foundation for defining *Elijah Muhammad Studies* identifying some of its goals as well as problems the field may face. The chapter also includes a short history of Elijah Muhammad. Chapter 2 deals with the major aspect of Elijah Muhammad's teachings which was the knowledge of God. This aspect of his teachings has caused considerable alienation from some religious leaders. Chapter 3 juxtaposes Elijah Muhammad's teachings with critical educational scholars. The chapter has a particular focus on the education of Black students. Chapter 4 examines the interdisciplinary scope of the teachings of Elijah Muhammad. This chapter contains direct quotes that are listed under various disciplines. The chapter provides a foundation for rethinking Elijah Muhammad within the disciplines of study.

Chapter 1

Goals, Challenges, and Misconceptions

Elijah Muhammad Studies is a field of study that examines the interdisciplinary scope of the teachings of Elijah Muhammad. The foundation for Elijah Muhammad Studies has its roots in the discipline of education. Elijah Muhammad implored that his mission was "to give life to the dead" (Muhammad, 1965). Thus his initial mission was to re-educate Black people, by providing them with knowledge, wisdom, and understanding that would restore them back into the nature in which they are created. While his work has implications that can be found in some schools and colleges of education, the profundity of his work is that it stretches across every discipline and field of study found at major research universities. In fact, most of these universities in their attainment of new knowledge are verifying what Elijah Muhammad taught in the 1930s.

Elijah Muhammad Studies introduces the interdisciplinary scope of Elijah Muhammad's teachings, with a specific focus on the discipline of education. It paves the way for new ground-breaking research that can elevate a new consciousness in the human being, thereby laying the foundation for a New World. In a world that is increasingly becoming more diverse and interdependent, the teachings of Elijah Muhammad should be re-examined as we prepare for the dispensation of new knowledge.

Goals of Elijah Muhammad Studies

The ever-increasing world violence is setting the stage for a New World. Elijah Muhammad Studies lays a foundation for examining Elijah Muhammad's teaching as we prepare for the New World that is on the horizon. A major goal of Elijah Muhammad Studies is to prepare scholars who can examine the teachings of Elijah Muhammad from their discipline or field of study. These scholars, while studying what is considered cutting-edge research, will hopefully come to find through comparative study in their respective areas of study that the teachings of Elijah Muhammad are essentially at the core of contemporary and ground-breaking research. It is hoped that once these scholars complete their comparative studies, they will be able to bring forth something new and completely different from what is considered ground-breaking research. Scholars in the field of Elijah Muhammad Studies are welcomed from diverse racial, ethnic, and religious groups. It is hoped that what will emerge from Elijah Muhammad Studies is *Elijah Muhammad Scholars* who will bring to birth a New World.

Unlike the scholarship in the current world, whereby the scholars are conducting new research, yet the minds of the scholars (and those who benefit from their scholarship) are still spiritually enslaved, Elijah Muhammad Studies explores the spiritual study of all fields and disciplines. What emerges from Elijah Muhammad Studies is the mind of God and his purpose for creation. The *Elijah Muhammad Scholars* are therefore engaged in the process of uncovering new research that will alter or change the mind of its adherents, thus releasing new ideas and thoughts. Ultimately it is hoped that Elijah Muhammad Studies will play a significant role in making "a new mind for us and a new way of thinking" (Muhammad, 1974, p. 123).

The primary goal of Elijah Muhammad Studies is to bring forth a New World from the genetic God coding already present in the human being. Its major goal is to produce a New World by awakening the God force in the human being. Elijah Muhammad points out:

> This is what he wants to make out of you and me, not just believers, but Gods. Every one of you according to what He has taught me will be Gods. (Hakim, 1997a, p. 272)

> For the new world you have a new education and government. The God of the New World is a New God. (Hakim, 1997b, p. 291)

It is ultimately the goal to produce *Elijah Muhammad Scholars* who can feed on the mind of God to disseminate *a new education.*

The Elijah Muhammad Student Scholar

The Elijah Muhammad Student Scholars comprise students who major in any discipline or field of study at higher education institutions. Over the course of studying the depth of Elijah Muhammad's teachings the students evolve into a new consciousness, thus stimulating new ideas. Elijah Muhammad Student Scholars have a commitment to bringing forth the God essence in the human being. The Elijah Muhammad Student Scholar is committed to the eternal principles of freedom, justice, and equality for the whole of humanity. Thus their research is one of service to humanity which moves beyond the search for materialism and fulfills the scriptural writing that says, "But seek first his kingdom and his righteousness, and all of these things will be given you as well" (Matthew, 6 vs. 33). Elijah Muhammad Student Scholars come from diverse backgrounds that transcend race, religion, class, gender, and ethnic divisions. It is ultimately the search for oneness with self, others, and the creator for the attainment of a New World.

Historical Look at Elijah Muhammad

Born Elijah Poole in Sandersville, Georgia, in October of 1897 to his parents, William and Mariah Poole, Elijah was one of thirteen children. The Pooles were sharecroppers in the Sandersville area. The name Elijah was given to him by his grandfather who had jokingly noted the significance of the name (Clegg, 1998). His mother however, felt the name accurately depicted the future greatness of the child that she had carried for nine months. Mariah had visions in which she was shown the future greatness of the child that she was carrying. Thus the name Elijah was paralleled with the Elijah of the biblical scripture. Elijah's childhood was centered on the family's work as sharecroppers in the area. Elijah was somewhat different from his siblings, which was highlighted by his ability to resolve differences that existed between them. His father was a Baptist minister in the local area and as a result he found himself listening, reflecting, and studying writings found in the Bible. The early education he received, like most Black people during that time period, was rooted in the teachings of the Bible. In *The Theology of Time,* he talked about his reluctance of joining the church at 14 because he didn't want to tell a lie by saying that God had told him to join. It seems as though he was born with a yearning for scriptural knowledge that would uplift his people from the cruelties of racism, hatred, and suffering inflicted upon them as a result of White supremacy. Elijah experienced first-hand the brutal legacy of White supremacy in the form of lynching. One of those experiences included an evening walk where he heard voices in the woods. He assumed that the sounds were his brothers who were out looking for him. As the voices got closer he realized that this was not his brother but in fact a group of white men who were leading a black man into the woods with a rope around him. Elijah fearfully observed the lynching of this man who attended his father's church. This along with the daily abuse by white supremacists probably caused Elijah to yearn for more knowledge, a knowledge that would provide a way out of the oppression suffered by Black people.

This terrible lynching experience along with other experiences would follow Elijah into Macon, Georgia. When Elijah was sixteen years old, he moved to Macon in search of work. There Elijah worked for the Cherokee Brick and Tile Company. In 1915, he met Clara Evans. Clara was one of three children in the Evans family. Clara's sister Rose recalled that Elijah, dressed in a blue suit, would visit their house on Sundays, where he would stay from around six to nine o'clock. After two years of courtship, Elijah married Clara on May 2, 1917 (Halasa, 1990).

Although Elijah witnessed the physical abuse of Blacks, Whites had never physically abused him. However, it has been mentioned that Elijah and his White employer had a dispute. The dispute led to what perhaps was a physical confrontation. It is not certain whether Elijah did any physical harm to his adversary. As a result of this confrontation, his mother may have feared for his life and pleaded with him to leave town (Farrakhan, 1996). This, in addition to the lack of jobs, was enough to force Elijah to move his family to Detroit. Elijah stated, "I have seen enough of the white man's brutality in Georgia to last me 26,000 years" (Halasa, 1990, p. 29).

Elijah could never have imagined what would await him when he reached Detroit. A common farm boy was about to enter into a journey of eternity, a destiny that awaited him before he was born. Elijah, like most Blacks who had journeyed north to find a better of way of life, was confronted with the false promises that so many had encountered in their journey. He had assumed that he would have been able to find work relatively easily; however, when this did not materialize he found himself drinking (Curtis, 2002; Farrakhan, 1996). Imagine what it must have been like for a young man coming from rural Georgia moving to the city of Detroit with a family. The anxieties and pressures that he and other Blacks faced would have been insurmountable for most people today. His drinking must have grieved his wife Clara as she reflected on the hopes that were unrealized, only to find themselves alone in a strange city. Elijah's drinking would be so bad that his wife would sometimes have to get him out of the alley where he had unconsciously fallen. He said that when God found him that only his eyeballs were out of the mud. Nevertheless, Clara had gone out to hear a man speaking in a hall. She later urged Elijah that he needed to come out and listen to this man. Elijah retorted that he was not interested in hearing heathenism, referring to Islam. Elijah was a devout Christian, son of a Baptist minister, student of the scriptures, probably assumed that he could never listen to this so-called heathenism. Reluctantly, after being given more information he decided that he would attend the meeting at Clara's request. Elijah could never have imagined that his world was about to change.

On September 22, 1931, he attended a lecture that he had some reservations about (Muhammad, 1996). As he listened to the presenter Wallace D. Fard, he reflected on the scriptural teachings that he had studied over the course of his entire life. He knew on an instant that this was the man that the scriptures said would come in the last days. I am not sure what Wallace D. Fard was teaching but I believe at the moment Elijah heard these teachings he immediately fell in love with the mysterious Wallace D. Fard. The scholars have pointed out that part of Elijah's acceptance of Fard's teaching was a result of his experiences in the South. This is probably true as those experiences were providing him with a love for the man that would come to be known as "the Savior." Once the meeting adjourned the custom was that Fard would shake hands with his listeners. The rendezvous with destiny was about take place, as Elijah shook hands with the man who would become his teacher, he replied "I know who you are; you are the one the Bible says would come in the last days under the name Jesus. Fard replied, yes but who knows this except yourself, be quiet." I wonder what Elijah must have felt like; perhaps he had come to realize that the yearnings that he felt since a child were now coming to pass. He had met the man that could provide a knowledge that would uplift his people. Elijah confirms, "Ever since he's [himself] been in his boyhood he's been craving to see someone come to the rescue of his people" (Hakim, 1997b, p. 27).

Within a month Fard sent a message out to Elijah that he could began teaching out in the Hamtramck area and that he would see him soon (Hakim, 1997b). Once their private meetings began Elijah was astonished by the knowledge that he received from the man who was known as W. D. Fard, later known as Wallace D. Fard Muhammad and currently referred to as Master Fard Muhammad.

Elijah pointed out that he studied under Master Fard Muhammad for 3 years and 4 months. Elijah explains this experience with Master Fard Muhammad by saying,

> Allah came to us from the Holy City Mecca, Arabia, in 1930. He used the name Wallace D. Fard, often signing it W.D. Fard. In the third year (1933), He signed it W. F. Muhammad which stands for Wallace Fard Muhammad. He came alone. He began teaching us the knowledge of ourselves, of God, and the devil, of the measurement of the earth, of other planets, and of the civilizations of some planets other than the earth.
>
> He measured and weighed the earth and its water; the history of the moon; the history of the two nations, black and white that dominate the earth . . . I asked him, Who are you, and what is your real name? He said, I am the one the world has been expecting for the past 2,000 years. I said to him again, what is your real name? He said, "My name is Mahdi: I am God, I came to guide you into the right path that you may be successful and see the hereafter. (Muhammad, 1965, pp. 16–17)

This relationship with Fard would spark a new beginning for Elijah Muhammad. For the next three-and-a-half years, Fard would teach Elijah on several topics ranging from theology, history, education, science, and numerous other topics. Elijah stated, "We used to sit sometimes from the early part of the night until sunrise and after sunrise" (Hakim, 1997b). Fard, according to Elijah Muhammad, was born on February 26, 1877, in Mecca, Arabia. Fard's birth was not what we would consider an ordinary process, as his father was in the circle of Gods who had come to the realization that some members of their family had been transplanted to United States of America. Fard's father, being of a very dark complexion, realized that he could not get among the people of America because the country was mostly white. As a result he went into the Caucasus mountains to find a white woman, to bear a child that would be fit to produce a son that could blend in among both groups of people (Black and White) and bring about justice. Muhammad would say regarding Fard's mother,

> He said his mother was a white woman. He said my father went up in the mountains to choose my mother in order to get a child that looked like the people that had this particular member among them, so that he could get among them more successfully, and that he was the one. His mother he said was a white woman, and his father was a black man. (Hakim, 1997b, p 45)

More importantly, was the fact that Fard had visited America for twenty years before making himself known. What I find most profound about Fard is that he studied and taught at a university in California and that he had enrolled at several other universities. Of major significance was that Fard studied every educational system in the civilized world, could speak 16 languages and write ten of them, and had extracted pictures of the people on Mars. Elijah Muhammad stated:

He studied every educational system in the civilized world and that he could speak 16 languages and write ten of them. He could speak 16 fluently. He said that he had been studying for us, what he meant to teach us, and reform us for forty two years. (Hakim, 1997b, p. 44)

The educational work of Fard is very significant as this is the root of Elijah Muhammad's educational philosophy. Fard, in studying every educational system in the civilized world and studying what he intended to teach the once slaves of America and eventually the human family, is giving us the keys to understanding the importance of proper education. Fard is also giving Elijah Muhammad his mission which was to teach a people who had been educated against the nature in which God had created them. Elijah Muhammad characterizes his mission by saying, "My work from him was to teach my people these facts, and reform them and make them what they should be; as they are children, the bible teaches, from God but they are lost in evil and practice evil" (Hakim, 1997b, p. 46). Elijah Muhammad reiterates the mission of education by saying his teacher said, "Tell them that I will walk up in a mountain 40 miles to teach just one of them. Tell them I love them" (p. 54). Elijah Muhammad's first major encounter with law enforcement officials was not a result of his teaching in the temple/mosque as had been customary, but it was for following through on the ultimate mission which was the establishment of schools that would grow the children into the mind of God.

In 1934, Elijah was charged with contributing to the delinquency of minors. The charge was a result of Muhammad's establishment of a school. The Michigan State Board of Education was probably fearful of the impact that a school related to the knowledge espoused by Muhammad would have on Black people, especially considering the controversy around Master Fard Muhammad. The teachers at the school were arrested first, and when Elijah discovered the arrest he committed himself to jail. The court gave Muhammad six-months probation and ordered that the children be placed back in public schools. Elijah did not meet this request. He knew the importance of setting up a school system that would allow individuals to grow into the knowledge of themselves. The mission given by his teacher was to teach (Muhammad, 1965; Hakim, 1997b). Elijah when describing his arrest refers back to the idea of developing a self-identity, which schools have refused to do both historically and contemporarily. As a result Elijah Muhammad sought to set up a system of education that would serve as the foundation for a new world. He reflected on the need for identity by describing his meeting with his teacher as a process that included deconstructing the names that Black people in America had assumed from their slave-masters. He pointed out,

The name Poole was never my name, nor was it my father's name. It was the name of the white slave master of my grandfather after the so-called freedom of my fathers. They, being robbed of the knowledge of self and kind, for the past 300 years did not know what deadly harm the slave-masters name would do to them in the way of true freedom and recognition among the free and independent nations of our own. (Hakim, 1997b, pp. 38–39)

This teaching by Fard and later by Elijah Muhammad required one to examine the self as a historical being who has been shaped by historical forces. These historical forces did not help Blacks in America to see who they really were in light of their history, origin, and purpose. Hilliard (2001) states the following with regard to the naming process: "At the conscious level, naming was a strategy to commit 'cultural genocide,' a strategy to destroy ethnic family solidarity, a strategy to place emphasis on individual rather than family behavior, or a strategy to confuse Africans about their ethnic identity" (p.10). What Elijah Muhammad taught was also noted by Dr. John Henry Clarke in the following words, "It is impossible to continue to oppress a consciously historical people" (Cited in Hilliard, 2001). In the context of understanding Elijah Muhammad, one must understand that his work reflected an educational process that would be truly transformative. To really grasp the teachings of Elijah Muhammad one has to delve into the background of his teacher [Master Fard Muhammad].

Several writers have tried to examine Fard Muhammad. They have pointed out that Fard was a criminal who was an imposter and that he had skillfully tricked Elijah Muhammad in his scheme to make money. *The Los Angeles Herald Examiner* in 1963 released an article along with a picture which they claimed was Wallace Dodd Ford who also went under the name Wallace D. Fard (Hakim, 1997b, Islam, 2007). The article highlighted that Wallace Dodd Ford had been arrested for drug use and several other crimes in California. Dr. Wesley Williams [aka True Islam] has painstakingly researched the claims that have been made in the *Los Angeles Herald Examiner* as well as a recent book, *The Messenger: The Rise and Fall of Elijah Muhammad,* as it relates to the claim that Wallace Dodd Ford is Wallace D. Fard. Williams in his book, *Master Fard Muhammad: Who is he? Who he is not?* carefully deciphers FBI documents concluding, "The story was hoax" (p. 25).

Despite this erroneous information that was used to discredit Elijah Muhammad some writers continue to use this misinformation as being reliable (Evanzz, 2001). The misinformation by these writers is a direct result of reliance on information that has come from those desiring to keep the masses away from Elijah Muhammad's true identity. The more recent attacks have come in the form of writers who passionately like to refer to the fact the Muhammad had wives. They point out that Muhammad while having programs that could uplift Black people he was in fact immoral. They report that he had affairs with his secretaries that were revealed in his rift with Malcolm X. They further explain that a major reason for Malcolm's split with the Nation of Islam was a result of his finding out about these "affairs." This aspect of Elijah Muhammad's life has been used as a basis to claim that he was immoral and could in no way be a messenger of God. Certainly Elijah Muhammad as he progressed through his mission assumed wives, his mission, and life experiences were key necessities in his reaching the ultimate plateau, oneness with God. Additionally, the domestic life of Elijah Muhammad parallels the life of Prophet Muhammad. Ghulan (1996) writing on the plurality of marriages by the Prophet Muhammad declares, "One of the most misunderstood aspects of the Prophet Muhammad's life has been the plurality of his marriages" (p. 123). While many have been critical of these marriages they demonstrate the depth of Muhammad's strength, knowledge, and character that supersede western ideas.

Eric Lincoln, one of the few writers to have personally studied Elijah Muhammad and the Nation of Islam, and author of one the first in-depth studies of the Nation of Islam has a different perspective from contemporary writers. Lincoln (1994) points out that,

> It is not unusual for religious groups to develop private ethics that may differ substantially from those of the "outside majority." Some Mormons, for example, and many Muslims are doctrinal polygamists, who remain committed to the "inside" practice of what they believe even if it is forbidden by the "outside law." Seen from this perspective, it seems unlikely that Malcolm X would have given serious consideration to defection from Elijah and the Nation of Islam over what must have been for him an issue of little consequence. (p. 262)

The media's play on words served as the springboard for the gross misinterpretation of Elijah Muhammad. Due to the lack of understanding regarding religious diversity among the masses of people in America it was easy for people to believe the propaganda. Another mechanism used to misinform the masses about Elijah Muhammad has come from *The Autobiography of Malcolm X*. In the book, it refers to Malcolm's disappointment with Elijah Muhammad, upon finding out about his wives. However, the reader is not given insight into who is doing the writing and for what purpose. Manning Marable, in his forthcoming book *Malcolm X: A Life of Reinvention*, reveals how *The Autobiography of Malcolm X* was the result of a government agent who knew of Alex Haley's dislike for the Nation of Islam, and as a result used Haley's dislike for the Nation of Islam and the rift between Elijah Muhammad and Malcolm X as the basis for the book's development. Manning in an interview pointed out the following regarding *The Autobiography of Malcolm X*:

> . . . most people who read the autobiography perceive the narrative as a story that now millions of people know, and it was—it's a story of human transformation, the powerful epiphany, Malcolm's journey to Mecca, his renunciation of the Nation of Islam's racial separatism, his embrace of universal humanity, of humanism that was articulated through Sunni Islam. Well, that's the story everybody knows. But there's a hidden history. You see, Malcolm and Haley collaborated to produce a magnificent narrative about the life of Malcolm X, but the two men had very different motives in coming together. Malcolm did—what Malcolm did not know is that back in 1962, a collaborator of Alex Haley, fellow named—a journalist named Alfred Balk had approached the F.B.I. regarding an article that he and Haley were writing together for The Saturday Evening Post, and the F.B.I. had an interest in castigating the Nation of Islam, and isolating it from the mainstream of Negro civil rights activity. So consequently, a deal was struck between Balk, Haley and the F.B.I. that the F.B.I. provided information to Balk and Haley in the construction of their article,

and Balk was—Balk was really the interlocutor between the F.B.I. and the two writers in putting a spin on the article. The F.B.I. was very happy with the article they produced, which was entitled, "The Black Merchants of Hate," that came out in early 1963. What's significant about that piece is that that became the template for what evolved into the basic narrative structure of The Autobiography of Malcolm X. (Retrieved from: http://www.columbia.edu/cu/ccbh/mxp/mxstun.html)

The book would serve as the needed propaganda, to discredit the work and mission of Elijah Muhammad. Another missing piece to the puzzle regarding Malcolm X's love for Elijah Muhammad, was that Malcolm had come to realize that he had been tricked by agents and that he and Elijah Muhammad were being pitted against each other by outside forces. Some people point out that Malcolm was in fact working on returning to the Nation of Islam. Marable (2007) alludes to this possibility when he describes Malcolm's desire to create an autobiography that would put him in the good graces of the Nation of Islam:

> Malcolm's objective was actually to reingratiate himself within the Nation of Islam, that because he had emerged by the early 1960s as a very prominent figure outside of the N.O.I., there were critics within the organization that were saying to the patriarch of the N.O.I., the Honorable Elijah Mohammad, that Malcolm planned to take over the organization, which was not true. But nevertheless, Malcolm felt that if he could make a public—a prominent public statement to show his fidelity to the Honorable Elijah Mohammad that that might win him back in the good graces of the organization. But there were internal critics, sharp critics, who were very opposed to him, and who were very—some of them were members of Elijah Mohammad's family, such as Herbert Mohammad, Raymond Shareef, who was the head of the Fruit of Islam, the brother-in-law of—the son-in-law of Elijah Mohammad. They isolated Malcolm X and kept him out of the newspaper of the organization Mohammad Speaks for over a year, which is kind of curious. He was the national spokesperson of the N.O.I., and he wasn't represented in their own newspaper for over a year. (Retrieved: http://www.columbia.edu/cu/ccbh/mxp/mxstun.html)

Marable also points out that the objective of Alex Haley was to produce a document that would ultimately smear the ideology of the Nation of Islam. Alex Haley and Malcolm X had two different objectives for writing the autobiography.

> Haley's objective was quite different. Haley was a republican. He was an integrationist. He was very opposed to black nationalism. His objective was to illustrate that the racial separatism of the N.O.I. was a kind of pathological or a kind of—it was the logical culmination of separatism and racial isolationism and exclusion. He wanted to show the negative aspects of the N.O.I.'s ideology, Yacub's history, and all of the ramifications of racial separatism that he felt were negative, and that Malcolm, being as charismatic as he was, a very attractive figure, nevertheless, he embodied these kind of negative traits. Haley felt he could make a solid case in favor of racial integration by showing what was—to white America—what was the consequence of their support for racial

separatism that would end up producing a kind of hate, the hate that hate produced, to use the phrase that Mike Wallace used in his 1959 documentary on the Nation of Islam. So, the two men for very different reasons came together. What is striking is that from almost from the very beginning of certainly by September and October of 1963, as the book was being constructed, that Haley was vetting—asking questions to the publisher and to the publisher's attorney regarding many of the things that Malcolm was saying. He was worried that he would not have a book that would have the kind of sting that he wanted. He was also concerned, to use Haley's phrase, about the purported anti-Semitism of Malcolm X, and so he began to rewrite words or passages in the book without Malcolm's knowledge. (Retrieved from website: http://www.columbia.edu/cu/ccbh/mxp/mxstun.html)

This new research shatters the credibility of the widely read autobiography of Malcolm X which has been a primary document used to analyze Elijah Muhammad and the Nation of Islam. Dr. Marable's research reveals the accuracy of the historical engineering referred to by Noam Chomsky. In the case of Elijah Muhammad and the Nation of Islam the historical engineering has resulted in a complete misunderstanding of one the most profound teachers the world has ever experienced. *The Autobiography of Malcolm X* has been able to keep the rift between the student and the teacher alive. Had Malcolm X been able to work his way back into the Nation of Islam, it would have been a terrible setback for those who had sought to destroy their relationship, the Nation of Islam, and the rise of Black people.

Ultimately, one has to enter into a course of study to determine the identity of Elijah Muhammad and the accuracy of the knowledge he revealed. We could enter into a long debate about Elijah Muhammad's personal life, but the most important thing that one must consider is how could a man with a fourth-grade education have a vast body of knowledge, wisdom, and understanding that is being used and verified in major universities. Daniel Burley makes a special note of the significance of Elijah Muhammad in the field of education: " . . . Muhammad, born Elijah Poole under the slave name of his parents, as Garvey had been before him, was particularly fitted to be a teacher of men. Not in the sense of the popular conception of the classroom teachers of rote and dogma, but in the classic molds of the great teachers of history—Socrates, Aristotle, Siddhartha Guatama, Guru Nanak, K'ung Fu-tze, Zoraster, Moses, Mohammed and Jesus Christ, most of whom were largely unlettered men" (Muhammad, 1965, p. xiii).

Perhaps the misunderstandings of Elijah Muhammad are problematic in this world because Elijah Muhammad's ideas signal the end of the modern world we are currently experiencing. Perhaps his critics should understand,

A man you can call him what you want to. Given a job, as I have been given, he can't take material things of this world to bring in as a foundation for another world. These things here in books and I have read, will not do for us to build a new world out of. We have to have new teachings. (Hakim, 1997b, p. 55)

Elijah Muhammad the unlettered man from rural Georgia has been thoroughly misunderstood by the masses. The knowledge, wisdom, and understanding that he revealed were only a preliminary message to get Black people in America moving. However, the impact of what he taught transcended Blacks in America, it had a profound impact on Muslims, Christians, Jews, Whites, Native Americans, Hispanics, Asians and others. More importantly his knowledge has come to be the basis for our technological advancements. As you read the following chapters you will see how Muhammad's knowledge compares and contrasts with scholars in a variety of disciplines.

Challenges to Elijah Muhammad Studies

Mis-representation

One of the major challenges that the field of Elijah Muhammad Studies will have to overcome is the simplistic historically engineered perceptions of Elijah Muhammad. Elijah Muhammad's pronouncements from their inception have threatened the ruling powers on every level. These ruling powers include religious leaders, governmental leaders, educational leaders, and scholars from diverse backgrounds. As a result of these powerful forces Elijah Muhammad has been misrepresented in the mass media and virtually locked out of any academic discussion that would lead to a truthful examination of his teachings and life mission. At a major elite university I was shocked to see a course titled: *The Failed Prophecies of Elijah Muhammad*. The course title reflects a lack of understanding and depth of what Elijah Muhammad taught. Prophecy can never be failed, because prophecy is simply history that has not occurred. In light of the current world situation, Elijah Muhammad's message is being fulfilled to the letter. Even the television documentaries that deal with prophecy have exclusively focused on what Europeans have said regarding the future world; however, Elijah Muhammad (1973), in his book *The Fall of America*, illuminates prophetical utterances beyond the scope of European visionaries. In addition, not only has Elijah Muhammad been obscure to the masses, some scholars (while claiming that their work is objective) use terminology to skew what Elijah Muhammad taught as a way of negatively influencing the unknowing reader. I have seen several writers refer to the teachings of Elijah Muhammad as mythology. In particular, they focus on concepts such as Yakub and the origin of White people; and the Mother Plane as mythological teachings. These shallow examinations do not really get into the science of Elijah Muhammad's teachings in any comparative way, as most of these writers have not really grasped the depth of what Elijah Muhammad taught. Thus a major challenge facing Elijah Muhammad Studies is the construction of knowledge. Banks (2008) points out that knowledge construction will help students understand, "how cultural experiences, biases, and values influence the knowledge construction process" (p. 64). The knowledge about Elijah Muhammad that is used in most institutions reflects the ideas of those in the ruling class (Watkins, 2001). The knowledge construction that has mis-represented Elijah Muhammad must be deconstructed. Elijah Muhammad Studies provides a way to construct a more accurate understanding of Elijah Muhammad, by providing a lens to compare and contrast the knowledge battle.

Hate Teachings

Another major challenge to Elijah Muhammad Studies is the 1959 documentary by Mike Wallace that mis-represented Elijah Muhammad's teachings as hate teachings. The documentary frightened the masses of people into a "hate Elijah Muhammad" phobia. This phobia was wisely architecturally designed to frighten those who would dare to study Elijah Muhammad's work as being labeled sympathizers of a hate monger. When in fact Elijah Muhammad's work gave White people a mirror to look at their actions and forced the ruling powers to reconstruct society in a way that Blacks would come to believe that White supremacy was destroyed through integration. The ruling powers were forced to change the openly racist actions that they adjudicated upon Black people. This ultimately led the White power structure to rethink their overt racist actions towards Blacks and others. If you were to go back 40 years ago, a short span of time, you would find White people openly displaying their hatred for Black people; however, within a short span of time these openly racist attitudes became hidden and in some cases destroyed. Today there are studies that are called White Studies. These studies have many similarities to what Elijah Muhammad taught regarding *whiteness*. Elijah Muhammad played a major role in shaping the current American society and in fact brought a knowledge that would destroy white supremacy and black inferiority.

Anti-Christian

One of the biggest mis-representations of Elijah Muhammad was that he was anti-Christian. This has led large numbers of people to have a fear of examining Elijah Muhammad's work. One of my students who is a Christian pointed out that he initially had a fear of reading about Elijah Muhammad because he felt it might sway his Christian beliefs. In his words he had to check how strong his foundation was before he began reading the book on the educational philosophy of Elijah Muhammad. Elijah Muhammad was not anti-Christian but was in fact against the western construction of Christianity. The western construction of Christianity was used to conquer and destroy original peoples all over the earth. Howard (2006) a White multicultural writer explains, "In addition to the devastating loss of life and land, the use of the Bible and Christianity as tools of oppression has been a particularly sad chapter in the establishment of White dominance" (p. 44). Peter McLaren (2007) a White critical educational scholar writes regarding western Christianity,

For many evangelical Christians the history of the United States is deeply prov-idential. For the increasing ranks of Americans who profess to serve no other king but Jesus, they see themselves as moral stewards of a country preordained by God to save humanity. Besotted with the white man's burden of uplifting the ignorant masses of the Third World so that they might join the ranks of the ci-vilized, evangelical Christians. (pp. 301–2)

Elijah Muhammad in attacking the European construction of western Christiani-ty was destroying the foundation of the White supremacy myth that was incul-cated in the masses. His attack on western Christianity was threatening to those in the highest positions of the Christian world who realized the truth in Elijah Muhammad's message. Thus propaganda had to be spewed, against Elijah Mu-hammad in a way that made it seem like he was against the teachings of Jesus. Elijah Muhammad defined Christianity and argued that he and his followers were the real Christians. Concerning being a Christian he wrote, "I'll tell you the true meaning of Christian which refers to us, the Muslims. 'Christian' means to be crystallized into one" (Muhammad, 1974, p. 50). The opponents of Elijah Muhammad used his deconstruction of western Christianity as a way to frighten the masses away from what he taught. For example when Elijah Muhammad declared that Christianity was a made-up, White man religion, the architects of Black thought immediately used these verifiable truths in an attempt to make Black Christians hate or dislike Elijah Muhammad. Elijah Muhammad forceful-ly declared the role of Europeans in shaping or altering the words of original scriptural texts. Ozmon and Craver (2008) in describing Thomas Aquinas pro-vide insight into how this altering took place,

In his monumental work *Summa Theologica*, Aquinas summed up the argu-ments dealing with Christianity and used the rational approach suggested by Aristotle in analyzing and dealing with various religious questions. As a matter of fact, many of the supporting arguments in Christian religion are derived from the work of Aquinas regardless of what branch of Christianity is consi-dered, and Roman Catholicism considers the philosophy of Thomas Aquinas (Thomism) to be its leading philosophy. (p. 45)

Throughout their text Ozmon and Craver provide deep insight into the European construction of western Christianity that verifies what Elijah Muhammad taught regarding the foundation of western Christianity. Again this is in no way arguing that Christianity is in itself bad, in fact the term Christianity, the idea of being crystallized into oneness with God in the eyes of Elijah Muhammad was a good thing. The question one would have to ask is: What kind of Christian? Elijah Muhammad (1974) posed this same question, "They say 'We are followers of Christ; that is why we call ourselves Christians.' Where are your works if you are following Christ? And who is Christ" (p. 50). As I look back on what Elijah Muhammad taught he seems to have put together a curriculum or type of jour-ney that would lead the student into submission (Islam) to ultimately gain one-ness and power (Christianity). His understanding of the diversity of religious beliefs made him see more deeply the new Islam (way of life) that would sweep the world.

Islamophobia

Another major challenge to Elijah Muhammad Studies is overcoming the misinformation about what is Islam. After September 11, 2001, conversations about Islam became widespread. Americans were eager to find out what was at the root of "this religion" (Islam) that seemingly caused so much death and destruction. Islamophobia gripped the nation and the world, setting the stage for violent attacks on Muslims or persons perceived to be Muslim. The attacks on Muslims who had middle-eastern characteristics resembled the attacks of Muslims under the teachings of Elijah Muhammad. Since the early 1930s the Nation of Islam has experienced vicious attacks in the form of outright murder, government surveillance, government interference, propaganda, and other distortions. The *Nation of Islam* has vehemently been attacked throughout its existence in America. Elijah Muhammad (1965) details these attacks in *Message to Black Man in America*

> Their record of unprovoked, evil attacks against our people is a long and vicious one. The attacks began in Detroit, Michigan, in 1932, 33 and 34 and from there to Chicago Illinois, April, 1935, and down to the attack and murder of the Muslims in Los Angeles, California, April 27, 1962. (pp. 216–17)

The recent wave of attacks on Muslims has concerned some multicultural scholars and moved them to address the issue of religious diversity in America's schools. The new multicultural education literature is providing prospective teachers and educators with some knowledge of Islam. Multicultural scholars in reworking their multicultural textbooks have devoted entire sections to the discussion of Islam (Banks, 2008; Bennett, 2003; Gollnick & Chinn, 2006). In an effort to make teachers conscious and more considerate of Muslim students, these multicultural scholars have opened the door for discussions about Islam, diversity, and education in the New World.

Banks (2008) highlights the significance of Islam, diversity, and its ever growing presence among Black Americans. He argues, "Religious diversity is increasing in the United States and in other nations around the world. . . . The fastest growing religion in the United States is Islam. Almost half of the growth in Islam is from converts; the majority of these converts are African Americans" (p. 18). Pipes (2000) points out that much of the credit for the spread of Islam among Black people in America is a result of Elijah Muhammad. In his article, *How Elijah Muhammad Won*, he expresses that Elijah Muhammad should take credit for the spread of Islam. He points out:

> It does not take much imagination to see that, should Islam in fact replace Christianity as the primary religion of African-Americans, this will have vast

significance for all Americans, affecting everything from race relations to foreign policy, from popular culture to issues of religion and state. Eric Lincoln, a leading authority on African-American Islam, once wrote that the Nation of Islam might "well change the course of history in the West." Should that come to pass, the credit, or blame, will belong above all to the "squeaky little man teaching hate," Elijah Muhammad. (P. 30)

While much is missing from the Pipes article regarding Elijah Muhammad, there is significance in what he has said regarding Elijah Muhammad changing the course of world history. Those in positions of real power realize this awesome truth and have taken great measures to deceive the world about the New World that is being forged from Elijah Muhammad. In fact, Elijah Muhammad declared the sun would one day rise in the West, symbolizing that the light of God would come from a despised and rejected people (Black people in America) in the West. Today we are face to face with all of the prophetic warnings and utterances of Elijah Muhammad. Muhammad boldly declared to the world that a new Islam would come into being, one that encompasses the entire spectrum of religious belief, touching humanity in all its diversity.

Islam according to Elijah Muhammad is not a religion, but it is the nature of God. He declares that if one were to study the first people they would not find a named religion. Referencing biblical text he argues that Adam and Eve did not declare a religion. The religion that could be found among Adam and Eve was to simply obey and submit to God. Religion from the teachings of Elijah Muhammad is not ritualistic as some would think but is in fact a way of life. Islam despite being formally declared after Christianity does not mean that it was nonexistent. According to *the teachings* of Elijah Muhammad, Jesus was a Muslim, and he declared this when he said his will and his father's will were one will. While much debate has been fueled regarding Christianity, Judaism, and Islam, Elijah Muhammad had a different outlook on the religious diversity that encompassed the world. His first effort was to first restore the *lost found* to their original way of life which is submission to God. Contrary to much of the argument that Elijah Muhammad was anti-Christian, he was in fact evolving into a Christian. To be Christian, according to many theologians, is to have power over the forces of nature, and to make one's will one with God. Elijah Muhammad described this process when he says, "When a righteous person becomes so righteous, gets close to God, God accepts him as his friend. Then the wills of each, is with each other and what one wills the other wills" (Hakim, 1997a, p. 180). Once one has been able to accomplish the goal of making the will(s) one they will come to peace, which is Islam. Muhammad (1965) declares, "Islam means entire submission to the will of Allah (God). It is moreover, a significant name. Its primary significance is the making of peace and the idea of 'Peace' is the dominant idea of Islam" (p. 68).

Positives for Elijah Muhammad Studies

There are several events that have laid a foundation for Elijah Muhammad Studies. The advancement in knowledge has made the teachings of Elijah Muhammad more acceptable to students studying in the universities. An example of this is the research that is taking place regarding life on Mars. When Elijah Muhammad declared that there was life on Mars in the 1930s, this probably sounded like something coming from a crazed man. However, at several major universities there are studies being conducted regarding life on Mars as well as other planets in our universe. Time seems to be shedding light on the truth of Elijah Muhammad's teaching. In addition, several universities have mission statements that are dedicated to social justice and the eradication of racism. The University of California at Santa Cruz is a unique university whose mission statement and vision seem to align with many of the concepts taught by Elijah Muhammad. This is also true of several other universities. The students and the scholars who study at these universities are unknowingly studying concepts taught by Elijah Muhammad. With the explosion in knowledge that has taken place at several universities across the world Elijah Muhammad Studies is poised to bring in the New World. The Elijah Muhammad Studies Scholars will be able to move beyond the current cutting edge research into the creation of new knowledge that originates from highest the plane of thought—the Originator.

Elijah Muhammad Studies and the New World

The deepening crises that are impacting our world today may give us the impression that there is no hope for a better future. The increase in world violence, natural disasters, wars, and rumors of wars is cause for major concern. For over 70 years, Elijah Muhammad proclaimed that this world is going out and that a new and better world was on the horizon. Kincheloe (2007) writes, "A better world is coming, schools based on a radical love can be constructed, and human suffering can be eased" (p. xvi). Today we are face to face with all of the warnings given by Elijah Muhammad. In introducing Elijah Muhammad Studies I am hopeful that this book will provide us with the ability to transcend the current crises affecting the world and project our minds into a New World.

The new world must first be brought forth by educing the genetic god coding within the human being. I call this achieving excellence through education. Here, *excellence* means that trait or superior quality that one genetically carries. The role of education is to bring forth that superior quality, giving the student purpose for existence. Elijah Muhammad clearly described this most important role of education by arguing that the job of the civilized man is to teach civilization. What are you waiting for? Learn all about yourself; it is your teacher's desire that you have luxury, money, good homes, and friendships in all walks of life. This can be accomplished through Elijah Muhammad Studies.

Chapter 2

The Knowledge of God

Curriculum developers point out that one of the essential questions to be asked in the development of curriculum is what knowledge is of most worth. Marsh and Willis (2003) contend, "at the basic level there are three kinds of questions to be asked, and these deal with the planned curriculum, the enacted curriculum, and the experienced curriculum" (p. 4). The three major questions to be considered are: 1) What knowledge is of most worth? 2) How should the curriculum be developed? and 3) How should the curriculum be experienced? (Marsh & Willis, 2003; Kliebard, 1995) In this chapter I examine the body of knowledge that Elijah Muhammad argued was the most important of all knowledge—the knowledge of God.

Elijah Muhammad began his educational program with the knowledge of God. He writes, "Of all the knowledge that one may have or obtain the knowledge of God is the greatest and most necessary of all knowledge" (Hakim, 2002, p. 17). Western philosophers of education were also concerned with questions of God, man, and the universe. Morris (1968) writes, "What is reality? Study of this central question is customarily carried on through study of other companion questions of essence: What is man? What is God? What is the Universe? What is knowledge, truth beauty, good, evil?" (p. 306) Elijah Muhammad answered these questions and more throughout his educational mission. In his book, *Message to the Black Man*, Muhammad points out that one of the biggest mental chains that deprived Black people in America of true freedom was their lack of knowledge into the reality of God. Muhammad challenged the root cause of the educational dilemma confronting Black people in America as being mis-educated about the reality of God. Muhammad (1965) pointed out,

> This teaching that of a mystery God enslaves the mind of the ignorant. My poor people are the victims of every robber. They are so pitifully blind, deaf, and dumb that it hurts, but I am going to prove to them that I am with Allah (God) and that Allah is with me, in spite of your ignorance of Allah and myself, whom he has sent. (p. 3)

Muhammad unlike any individual or group redefined the concept of God. Muhammad pointed out that God is a man. The following points illustrate Muhammad's ideas about God and man when he says, "God is a man and we just cannot make him other than man lest we make him an inferior one; for man's intelligence has no equal other than man. His wisdom is infinite capable of accomplishing anything that his brain can conceive" (Muhammad, 1965, p. 6). This teaching was revolutionary as the masses of people all over the earth, and even those who were Muslims were shocked by Muhammad's proclamation that God is a man. Berg (2009) writes, "Most other Muslims believe in the absolute oneness and uniqueness of God (which precludes God taking any human form) . . ." (p. 3). Dr. Wesley Williams (a.k.a. True Islam) to the contrary of most Islamic scholars writes that the notion of God being a man can be found in ancient scriptural text: "Within this atom the creator-deity now resided and, eventually, from this atom he emerged as a luminous *anthropos* (man), the so-called sun god: Atum-Re of Eygpt and Prajapati-Brahma of India" (p. 168). Thus the notion of God being a man can be discerned by researching ancient texts. The teaching of God being a man is the foundation of Elijah Muhammad's educational program.

This teaching—God is a man—has varying degrees that must be understood. One aspect related to the concept that God is a man deals with a self-reflective process that requires one to think more deeply about the powers within oneself. The more the individual reflects on knowledge in relation to self they are able to develop a new consciousness that empowers them. The self-reflective process is needed in the education process. It is particularly important for oppressed people who have historically been denied the right to proper education.

Education in America has been framed with the opposite goal in mind. The self-reflective process is null and void in the current educational setting that is driven by high stakes testing. A scientific management approach to education is at the forefront of education. Thus, education follows a factory model of producing better workers for corporate capitalist interest. Bowles (cited in Noel, 2008) identified this as social reproduction, arguing that "unequal schooling reproduces the social division of labor" (p. 21) —preparing students for their roles in the larger society. Elijah Muhammad (1965) addressing the social reproduction theory writes, "My people should get an education which will benefit their own people and not an education adding to the 'storehouse' of their teacher" (p. 39). Elijah Muhammad is arguing that the education of Black people has not really benefited them as a group but has a reproductive function of adding to the "their teacher" meaning those who have shaped the society, schools, and curriculum—Whites in positions of power. The continued European dominance of schools and curriculum creates a plethora of problems for students in public schools. In particular, a large number of Black children are being impacted in a negative way. One of the leading concerns for educators is how to close the achievement gap that exists between Black and White students.

The scholars of education have pondered over the teaching strategies and instructional programs that are needed to help Black children to become equally successful as their White peers, but none of their programs have touched the surface of what Elijah Muhammad espoused. Critical educational theorists have identified one aspect of what is needed to make schools just and equitable in articulating that there must be an examination of knowledge and power (Apple, 2004; McLaren, 2007). However, Elijah Muhammad, with the concept that God is a man, is breaking the entire system of educational thought, because he is exposing the human potential that lies dormant in the human being as a result of

White supremacy. Once the student comes to an understanding that God is a man this will unlock human potential within and serve as a spring board for un-limited growth. Furthermore, Muhammad is shattering the foundation of power and knowledge prescribed by those in power—ending what he called the slave and master relationship.

The most noted scholars in the field of educational theory would probably have problems with the teaching that God is a man, just like the masses of people. In fact, the mention of God and education can become controversial de-spite the fact that western education was built on ideas about God. Today God and education seems to be a moot point in education discourse. Akbar (1998) explains the difficulty of separation of church and state for European American culture,

> The conflict is a consequence of the rigid separation between church and state which has been established in their conception of education. They also maintain a strong separation between the rational and the spiritual that actually fuels a continuing conflict between spiritual and scientific knowledge. (p. 50)

The topic of God is something that the majority of the educational scholars at-tempt to stay away from. It is as though their ideas are unrelated to their beliefs.

Let us consider for a moment the debate about God. While this debate about God seems to be centered around ideology and practice of worship, Muhammad had an entirely different concept of God. Muhammad's concept was completely opposite from the debate that is taking place in schools and the larger society. Muhammad begins by answering the question: What does it mean when we say God? Muhammad explains that when we use the term God we are saying know-ledge, force, and power. This according to Muhammad means that whoever has the greatest degree of knowledge ultimately has the force and power to rule dur-ing that period, thus becoming the God. Muhammad points out,

> God is a man, a flesh and blood being, but he is a Divine Being. Why do we call God a Divine Being? Because He is a Being like we are but His wisdom, power and other capacities and attributes are Supreme, making him the Highest Power . . . He has the Divine Power to will whatever He wishes and to bring it into existence with His Divine Will. (Lomax, 1962, p. 127)

> We want you to know God and teach you what God does. God means some-thing of Power, Wisdom, Knowledge and Understanding. That's a God who's superior to others. His knowledge of the creation is so deep into the visibility of things, we look upon him as having the power to make things do what he want them to do, because the father is our own kind. (Hakim, 1997a, p. 272)

Elijah Muhammad's disclosure of God and education is rooted in a concept that transcends a ritual. The ideas of Elijah Muhammad are rooted in those things that schools are supposed to provide—which are knowledge, wisdom, under-standing, and power. If schools incorporated his teachings, one has to wonder how the communities that serve Black, Hispanic, Native Americans, the poor, and the masses would be transformed. These communities would be transformed as the very basis for a new thought which would be inculcated in the students, thus causing a revolution. It would fulfill Muhammad's goal of making Gods. Muhammad explains the process of this revolution in education:

> How must the God of righteousness begin? What thought do you have of him and his beginning? He makes all things new. The first way to bring about something new is to change the way of thinking of the people. When you have removed from the people the old mind and idea then you can insert new ideas into their minds. This is done by the old being attracted by a new way of teaching . . . a new school of learning to condition their minds to that thing that you are about to present to them that is altogether new and different from what they have been accustomed to. (Hakim, 1997b, p. 289)

This kind of teaching is revolutionary in the fullest sense because Muhammad is talking about a new school of teaching and learning. He is not talking about how to integrate or fix the educational problem, but rather how to bring into existence that which no one has seen. Students under this type of educational system will develop new ideas which will serve as the basis for creating a new world. Additionally, his teachings provide a springboard for the creation of new ideas when he says that God created himself from matter that he took out of the darkness. What does this mean with regard to human potential? Do we have the same ability to create something out of the darkness? What can we bring forth from the darkness? The knowledge espoused by Elijah Muhammad is light—likened unto the sun, which would give life to students-causing them to evolve into a new being. Farrakhan (2006) explains,

> There's matter in the darkness. It is considered nothing because it has neither form nor function, but it's matter. So, now He's forming. As he forms himself, he studies himself. Then he makes a reality that corresponds to himself. Well, later he said let there be light. There was already light in Him. The Honorable Elijah Muhammad says, "He was a light of Himself." So what he did was bring out of himself a reality and put it in a beautiful form and gave it purpose to manifest who he is. (p. 263)

This is the essence of education. Since education is about a bringing forth or leading out, this could mean that each of us was brought into existence from the mind of the Creator for a very specific purpose, which is to demonstrate the presence of God within us. However, these thoughts must be developed or mined out of the individual otherwise those thoughts would remain hidden or in the darkness of consciousness. To be effective, education must bring these thoughts out of the darkness into a visible vision in our minds. Proper education will make manifest to our conscious mind ideas that will illuminate our purpose for existence. This turns on the lights, giving us vision, inspiration, motivation, and purpose, which will give rise to a beautiful form and demonstrate the power of God in the human being.

God and School

The very essence of schooling is rooted in the idea of God, but what God. Schools have struggled with the controversy around the issue of religion and God for years. Some of the more recent debates have stemmed from evolution and intelligent design to prayer in school. Spring (2006) briefly describes the debate regarding creationism and intelligent design theory, "Creationism maintains that humans did not evolve but were created as part of an intelligent design of the Universe. Creationist ideas are also called abrupt appearance theory or intelligent design theory" (p. 309). The debate regarding religion has also included issues regarding prayer in school. Despite the *No Child Left Behind Act's* section on school prayer, which allows for "school prayer within boundaries of the law," most public schools still grapple with issues related to prayer in school (Spring, 2006). Most school systems have supposedly attempted to make schools neutral with regards to religion. Pitre (2008) contends that when Black students are forced to say the Pledge of Allegiance and sing patriotic songs with the reference to God they are being taught that patriotism is closeness to God. In addition, he points out, "this along with the idea of modern schooling replacing the church put those ruling powers who shape education directly in charge of the moral values that are instilled in children, which ultimately leads to a continuous cycle of manipulation and control" (p. 36). Macedo (cited in Chomsky, 2000) uses the term theological to explain the role of school in indoctrinating students for benefit of the ruling class. The debate regarding the separation of church and state reinforces Akbar's analysis of the Euro-centered approach to education for Black students. Akbar correctly points out, "The African worldview does not approach the study of God as some kind of force independent of the human reason and physical reality. Instead it sees God as an inescapable component of human life" (p. 50). The assumption by the masses who are indoctrinated with a Euro-centered perspective is that we are here to learn our subjects and the idea of God is not necessary. However, under close examination the ideas of religion and the belief in a God are fundamental to the educational process. The idea of who is providing the knowledge base and for what purpose ultimately signifies who is the ruler or God of that time period. So in the minds of those who control education and society the debate about God does not matter as long as they continue to shape the ideas of young people to serve their interest. Ultimately they realize they are the Gods regardless of the people's belief. Farrakhan (2006) explains this concept by saying "If a man controls what goes in, he can control what comes out. He who sets the diameter of your knowledge determines the circumference of your activity" (p. 20). This also means the man who controls the circumference of your activity becomes the God of your activity as you will be limited to his ideas. One has to ask the question: What is the activity that is taking place in and around schools that serve large numbers of poor students, but in particular Black children, in the inner cities of America? Kozol writes, "In Boston, the press referred to areas like these as 'death zones'—specific reference to the rate of infant death in ghetto neighborhoods—but the feeling of the 'death zone' often seemed to permeate the schools" (Cited in Noel, 2008, p. 32). The schools and the surrounding communities represent death and the schoolhouses reproduce what exists in the larger society. This recycling of death coincides with the earlier discussion of social reproduction theory. Nieto and Bode (2008) explain,

> According to this theory, the role of schools was to keep the poor in their place by teaching them the proper attitudes and behaviors for becoming good workers, and to keep the dominant classes in power by teaching their children the skills of management and control that would presumably prepare them to manage and control the working class. Schools, therefore, reproduced the status quo and not only reflected structural inequalities based on class, race, and gender but also helped to maintain these inequalities. (p. 260)

In order to disrupt the reproductive function of schools students must have a body of knowledge that causes them to overthrow the internalized oppressor consciousness. The knowledge of God starts this process of knocking out the oppressor consciousness by opening up another side in the human being. It creates a vision of education that supersedes the current paradigm of education. It is an education to produce Gods—freeing human beings to realize the self-dwelling attributes of the creator. Elijah Muhammad summarizes the goal and outcome of this kind of knowledge,

> This is what he wants to make out of you and me, not just believers, but Gods. Every one of you according to what he has taught me will be Gods . . . We have power if restored to what we originally were, but we have been robbed of power through being deprived of the knowledge of self. Just think about it, you're bowing to the creature instead of the creator; you are far off. You are from the creator and this is a creature of the creator. You are also the brother of the creator; you should be able to create. (Hakim, 1997a, p. 272)

The concept of being a descendant of God and having the same power to do what God does will bring about a new person. The knowledge of God as taught by Elijah Muhammad would start a process whereby the educational system would seek to pull out that which is within. Akbar (1998) calls this educing, which is rooted in the term education, "In order to become really human our humanity must be educed, brought forth or brought out" (p. 2). This bringing forth will give the student purpose, direction, and power—creating a New World.

Creation and Education

The idea of being able to create is one of the main handicaps of public education. The idea of being able to create demonstrates another aspect of the relationship between power and knowledge. If the majority of people have been primarily consumers of others ideas then the essence of the God force has not been educed. Therefore the greater potential to transform the self has not been accomplished making the educational process limited. Woodson (1999) describes this dilemma which continues to impact Black education when he says, "The Negro will never be able to show his originality as long as his efforts are directed from without by those who socially prescribe him. Such friends will unconsciously keep him in the ghetto" (p.28). To create according to Muhammad is the very essence of God. Muhammad says that, "This is like the creation of us. In the beginning, the God who created us had no material to use to begin his creation. He had only himself. Therefore out of darkness and the thoughtless and invisible he brought out the visible vision and idea" (Hakim, 1997b, p. 290). Muhammad further explains that God in the creation of himself did not have a model or pattern to start his creation,

> It took an architect to design the universe. Our first father formed and designed himself. Think over a man being able to design his own form and he never saw another man before he saw himself. Powerful! (Hakim, 1997a, p. 273)

The idea of creating forces one to think about our ability to create, control and master obstacles and barriers that deprive us from becoming Gods. Creating requires one to envision that which does not exist, to ultimately bring forth something new. We must ask critical questions about creating and its relationship to education.

Muhammad used the zero to explain the creating process. He starts by detailing how God started from nothing to begin his creation. If we examine the zero it forms a circle, it is also the number which we start at to produce the other numbers. Zero according to Muhammad serves as a base to understand our evolution from nothing to something. Muhammad notes:

> I only want to bring you into the knowledge of yourself. Why are you nothing? Are you in any way tallied with universe? Yes. "Elijah why did you make the zero round?" Because that's the way the universe was before the creation of man. Out of it we came by one who was self created. He didn't come from the creation of another. He's the self creator himself—The first—remember that. He made himself in a circle so that the wisdom of his self-creation could keep going to give knowledge, wisdom, and understanding to you and me. I want us to remember that . . . Out of the darkness came one and then he took the unknown and put it in front of himself. For what? To produce the known. That's why zero goes in front. To make more zeros, he puts more up beside zero and it keep producing or making this "one" ten-fold more powerful than it is by just adding zero's. (Hakim, 1997a, p. 68–69)

Thus, curriculum should be designed to help students connect to their creative mind. This means that a major outcome of education should be how well students can create.

Elijah Muhammad answered questions that the early philosophers of education posed. Theories about man, the universe, and God are the foundation for the current educational system that is depriving the majority of human beings of their human right to develop the God power within themselves. The current corporate capitalists' scripted education kills creativeness. Elijah Muhammad unlike philosophers and theorists brought a definitive teaching that if carefully studied by the masses would change their lived reality. Skillfully, he built his educational system and the Nation of Islam on the knowledge of God. He started his curriculum around the question, who is God? Answering this question would create a well of knowledge.

When the question of God, man, and the universe is answered, education takes on a totally different meaning. What can we create? Is there anything that is impossible? Elijah Muhammad answered these questions by saying yes you can create and nothing is impossible. Since we are from the creator, schools should help us to develop our essence, which is rooted in creating. When properly educated into our essence we will begin to seek knowledge, wisdom, and understanding. Nothing is impossible according to Elijah Muhammad when God created himself in the darkness, he destroyed the impossible. Thus, we should start the process of building a New World—one that helps us reach unlimited heights. Jesus when asked by his disciples when will the kingdom of God come? Replied the kingdom of God does not come with your careful observation because the Kingdom of God is within you. Elijah Muhammad's mission was to raise the God force in the human being.

Chapter 3

The Knowledge of Self

Without a doubt, Elijah Muhammad is one of the most influential men to have ever lived. His mission, work, and teachings have been the subject of voluminous research. Unlike any who came before him, Elijah Muhammad outlined what knowledge was needed to emancipate and resurrect the Black mind. Integral to this goal was that Black people in America attain the knowledge of self, which would lead them to become gods. Muhammad paid specific attention to the fact that schools did not provide Blacks with an in-depth knowledge of self; in his view, even "Negro history week" did not go far enough in giving Black people the knowledge needed to become gods.

Although Muhammad's teachings seemed very radical at the time, they are similar to those of scholars who have been termed *critical educational theorists*. Elijah Muhammad was not an educational theorist; however, his work allows us access to the most profound knowledge ever given to humanity: the knowledge of self, the knowledge of God, and the knowledge of the time. These three components comprise what may be termed the *light*.

Farrakhan (2006) describes the oneness of knowledge and light: "wherever there is knowledge, knowledge is light and light is power. Light causes the Earth to spin, so light makes revolution or revolt" (p. 10). Proper knowledge is the key to revolution or change. Lloyd (1998), paraphrasing Spinoza, discusses the significance of the knowledge of self and God:

> . . . there are things more important than a long life; that change from an infant body to a corpse is not the epitome of unhappiness; that a long life spent without the knowledge of self, God and of things may be a more unhappy outcome than early death. (p. 157)

Muhammad's mission was not to create helpless beings but to create gods. As he clearly articulates, "[God] wants to make out of you and me, not just believers, but Gods" (Hakim, 1997b, p. 272). Unfortunately, the majority of the research on Elijah Muhammad has not fully grasped the depth of his work. Several scholarly works have not been able to penetrate the surface to extract the essential core teachings of Elijah Muhammad. Even more disheartening is the fact that some researchers have clearly attempted to distort Elijah Muhammad and his teachings. This may be in part because of the magnitude of change that Elijah Muhammad's teaching represents to the ruling powers, ultimately ushering in a change—a whole new era—for humanity.

Despite the negative media attention, some scholars have noted Muhammad's greatness and his significant contribution to education. James Banks, one of the leading scholars in education and considered by some to be the founder of multicultural education, wrote about the Nation of Islam in 1973 and its positive impact within the Black community. In an edited book, *Teaching Ethnic Studies: Concepts and Strategies,* Banks (1973) writes, "The Nation of Islam has been able to provide many Blacks educational and job opportunities" (p. 162). In a recent conference on *Educating Black Boys,* Dr. James Moore of Ohio State University acknowledged the significance of Elijah Muhammad and the Nation of Islam in educating Black people, noting, "Let's look at the Nation of Islam. How can they take someone the world has thrown away and transform them from the inside and the outside?" (Muhammad, 2008, p. 12) Clearly, there are scholars who see the importance of Elijah Muhammad and his work.

In this chapter, I examine knowledge of self, multicultural education, critical pedagogy, separate schools, critical race theory, and critical white studies. It is from these various concepts that Elijah Muhammad Studies offers the possibility of creating something new.

Knowledge of Self

Elijah Muhammad introduced a body of knowledge and curriculum proven in its ability to transform people beyond race, class, or gender. Evidence is seen in Muhammad's students, who came from a wide range of racial and ethnic groups, including Native Americans, Hispanics, Asians, and Whites. Dorothy Fardan, a White scholar, noted, "I never felt Elijah Muhammad offended me for telling the truth; I felt he saved me from falsehood" (p. 13).

Muhammad and Woodson both believed that the education of Black people in America must include historical knowledge of Black people. Through a process of mis-education, Black people in America have historically been rendered blind, deaf, and dumb. The only way to reverse this cyclical mis-education is to trace the history of man, beginning with the question, "Who is the original man?" The answer to this question is the basis for the knowledge of self.

Elijah Muhammad taught the "original man is the Asiatic black man, the maker, the owner, the cream of the planet Earth, God of the universe." Muhammad (1965) explains, "We find history teaches that the earth was populated by the black nation ever since it was created but the history of the white race actually does not take us beyond 6,000 years" (p. 53). Social scientists have confirmed that the oldest humans lived in Africa. In their search for the origins of man, Louis and Mary Leakey in 1959 (Spivey, 2003) unearthed the oldest human fossil remains in Africa. Years later in 1974, Donald Johanson discovered the fossilized remains of a female hominid that came to be named Lucy. Lucy's gene pool has been traced back to East Africa and is believed to be slightly less than 3.18 million years old (Retrieved from: Institute of Human Origins). Without ever making a trip to East Africa, Elijah Muhammad argued that the history of the Black man dated into the trillions of years; so far in fact, that there would be no way to trace the origin of the Black man because it began when God created Himself in triple darkness. Thus, the Black man has no birth record:

> If we see that one emerged out of all this darkness, what force or power in the darkness brought it out? . . . The one was already in the darkness but could not be given to us until time brought it about, it emerged in our view into a revolving life that was hidden in darkness. We don't know how many trillions of years it was there, but it was there. It made itself of a fine atom of water that it found out there with it in the darkness of the universe. We could not see life emerging out of space without water because we can't produce life without water. Therefore there is some water out there in that darkened world. (Rassoull, 1992, pp. 97–98)

Elijah Muhammad explained the origin of the Black man more profoundly than scholars and scientists who came after him could. In fact, as recently as 1996 scientists confirmed that "In a stellar cloud 25,000 light years from the earth, researchers have found ordinary vinegar, an organic molecule that may have played a role in the formation of life" (Associated Press, 1996).

Elijah Muhammad raised the question of man's origin to inspire his students to rethink their identity. In helping Blacks to develop a true identity, Muhammad's work fulfilled W.E.B. DuBois' (1982) yearning for relief from the *double consciousness* that affected Black people, explained as:

> . . . a peculiar sensation . . . this sense of always looking at one's self through the eyes of others, of measuring one's soul by the tape of a world that looks on in amused contempt and pity. One ever feels his twoness—An American, a Negro; two souls, two thoughts, two unreconciled strivings; two warring ideals in one dark body, whose dogged strength alone keeps it from being torn asunder. (p. 45)

DuBois went on to express a desire to attain "self conscious manhood," which Okafor (2006) explains thus:

> By self conscious manhood Du Bois means that the African in America aspires to have freedom and liberty to reside in the polity called the United States as an African without being subjected to harassment. The African, he avers, neither wants to Africanize America nor become a White American. The African, he posits, now understands the way by which she could occupy her rightful place in the American scheme of things is by being herself and not someone else. (p.115)

Elijah Muhammad similarly posits, "Accept your own and be yourself." He writes,

> It is an act of intelligence and love for us to accept our own. One will say, "What is our own?" No. 1 our own people—our own earth, God and his religion, Islam (the religion of peace) and our own place in the sun. This divine

call to us to accept our own makes sense. Everything of life will accept its own kind. (Muhammad, 1965, pp. 50–51)

Elijah Muhammad taught Black people's identity is rooted in the self-creation of God. This propelled Muhammad's students to conduct more in-depth research on the knowledge of self.

Today, the knowledge of self is needed more than ever before. With the culture war that has been produced by social engineers, the Black community is continuously being attacked with silent weapons more harmful than the psychological impact of slavery. In addition, the new standardization of education has limited the discourse necessary to resurrect the Black mind. Four-hundred-plus years after the institution of slavery, Black people are still victims of amnesia, which for Muhammad (1965) was critical evidence of the need for the knowledge of self:

> I am for the acquiring of knowledge or the accumulating of knowledge—as we now call it education. First, my people must be taught the knowledge of self. Then and only then will they be able to understand others and that which surrounds them. Anyone who does not have a knowledge of self is considered a victim of either amnesia or unconsciousness and is not very competent. The lack of knowledge of self is a prevailing condition among my people here in America. Gaining knowledge of self makes us unite into a great unity. Knowledge of self makes you take on the great virtue of learning. (p. 39)

Schools have purposely left out any real discussion of the history of Black people. A few years ago school controversy erupted over a Louisiana school's Black History program that empowered students to move beyond gang violence, drug use, low test scores, and student resistance to school (Pitre, Ray, & Pitre, 2008). In the book, *Struggle for Black History: Foundations for a Critical Black Pedagogy in Education*, one student from that school explained the transformative power of Black History:

> Well, by the time that program had come about all of that [territorial fights] was put to an end. Because there was a teacher at our school, he was a new teacher, he came straight out of college. And at that time, around '92 or '93 there were territorial fights every day, I mean 15 to 20 people fighting every day. But I mean, when this teacher got there he started to work with the guys who were fighting. And, you know, letting them know that you really don't have anything to be fighting about. And all of that was to be no more, I mean these same guys were at the Black History Program dressed in suits and ties, [they] were from rival communities and they were like walking and talking to each other because they played a major role, a big part in the organization of the Black History program.

> And that is what led us to wanting to have someone from the Nation of Islam [as a guest speaker]. Because these guys they were on to something; one day they were fighting and the next day they were almost holding hands. They were really feeling close to one another and that was culmination of them being able

to tolerate one another. They were becoming friends . . . they were friends. I think a lot of people took something away from the program and for the most part it was a new self-respect. Those guys who had dressed in the suits and who were from town X and town A, who could not get along at the beginning of the year, they were setting an example. Because everybody knew that those guys just couldn't get along and we saw them dressed in ties, suits, and nice shoes. And they were standing there with order and discipline. We said, you know, they have something, because any time you can take somebody who's fighting one day and have them cooperating and being friends the next day, you have accomplished something. And I think a lot of people took that away from the program. We don't have to be disorderly, you know, we can get along and we can have pride in ourselves and in our school. It doesn't have to be a ruckus all the time. (p. 51)

Another student pointed out the necessity of critical Black History as the vehicle for unity:

. . . We realized that the reason we were fighting each other was because we were ignorant and we didn't want to learn from each other. Every one of us could bring something to the table. And maybe what was going on in my home wasn't going on in somebody else's, but maybe [there was] something that I could learn from that. At one time we weren't seeing eye to eye, but with the help of that instructor, the teacher, we learned that we could get along, [and] because of that we became good friends. So we learned that being together, we were very powerful. What one of us was lacking, the other made up for, so we realized that we could voice our opinion to the principal and the school board and we just had to suffer the repercussion[s]. And what we believed was that we had something concrete. (p. 59)

Elijah Muhammad pointed out that the unity of Black people would be more powerful than a nuclear weapon, and the students of this particular high school experienced part of that empowerment and unity that is the byproduct of knowledge of self. Today, signs of disunity among Black students are visible in urban schools. Oft times, these students attend separate schools and are caught up in such rivalry that they are driven to violence against others simply for being from different neighborhoods. Proper education would lead to the development of unity among these students so they could begin the process of addressing the problems that confront their communities. In fact, too many Black students do not understand how the present has been shaped by the past, or as Woodson (1999) calls it, the "seat of trouble," a lack of historical understanding:

These things must be viewed in their historic setting. The conditions of today have been determined by what has taken place in the past, and in a careful study of this history we may see more clearly the great theatre of events in which the Negro has played a part. (p .9)

This amnesia state has clearly been detrimental to Black students; thus, Elijah Muhammad stressed, "know thyself." Muhammad's (1965) students were inspired to seek knowledge because he espoused that "No followers, nor any other people, are more zealous about the acquiring of knowledge than my followers" (p. 39).

Elijah Muhammad accurately describes the necessity of the knowledge of self as the stimulus that inspires students to begin the journey for more knowledge. It is the knowledge of self that propelled Muhammad's students to become intellectual giants. I often hear teachers ask what is needed to inspire students. Muhammad knew that the answer lies in the knowledge of self. To really understand what he meant, we must explore more deeply by asking the following: What is the knowledge of self? How does the knowledge of self apply to an educational setting?

The knowledge of self is a process whereby the student is put on a journey that will ultimately lead to the discovery of his or her purpose. That knowledge will begin to unravel as the student embarks on the journey of self-transformation. This journey of self-transformation begins with cleaning up the faculties of the human mind. Throughout his mission, Elijah Muhammad's teaching appeared to some as only a non-descript religious teaching, but he was ultimately providing his students with valuable spiritual precepts. I define the term *spiritual* as "scientific teaching that involves uncovering the origin or nature of the human being." Spiritual teaching leads to a discovery of power that is unseen; thus, students of Elijah Muhammad must gain knowledge of self that deals with both the physical and spiritual. As students begin to immerse themselves into the knowledge of self, they develop a desire for more knowledge.

Following Muhammad's teachings ultimately leads to a physical discipline where the student is asked to refrain from certain foods that will hinder them in the goal of reaching their true potential. In his writings, Muhammad detailed the significant power of food: "He [Master Fard Muhammad] taught us that the slave masters had taught us to eat the wrong food and that this wrong food is the cause of our sickness and short span of life" (p. 17). On one hand, Muhammad's illustration of harmful food represents the physical food that we feed our bodies, but on the other hand he also means the food that we feed our minds. As the student begins to purge himself of harmful foods and ingests only those that nourish both the mind and body, he or she begins to uncover mental powers that they had never known to exist. The discovery of mental powers is a major aspect of the knowledge of self, and it leads to the further discovery of the student's mind.

Upon first meeting Fard Muhammad, Elijah Muhammad was tasked with reading 104 books that served as the impetus for knowledge of self. As Elijah Muhammad pursued this course of study, the language of one of these texts so impressed him that he felt he was looking at a picture of himself within its pages. Muhammad thereafter argued that if each of us studied intensely, we could also find a picture of ourselves in a book. Muhammad the student was constantly growing into a greater understanding of himself. Ultimately, he attained a level of thought that made it possible for him to discuss his revelatory knowledge of the origin of the universe. Muhammad's knowledge of self was constantly evolving—so much so that he ultimately came to understand, in a very profound way, how to conquer death. Thus his knowledge of self had been completed on one level and he discovered another innately human power that answers the ultimate reason for education. The ultimate reason for education is to conquer death.

There are plants that have the ability to regenerate themselves through the process of death. Scriptural writings refer to this very process: "Unless a kernel of wheat falls to the ground and dies, it remains only a single seed" (John 12:24, NIV). This saying has profound scientific implications, which Elijah Muhammad discovered through his journey to knowledge of self. Thus, the knowledge of self is a course demanding the student to be ever-evolving into his or her purpose for existence. Tynnetta Muhammad (2001) posits that the lessons presented by Elijah Muhammad are much more than recitation; they involve a process of travel leading to higher planes of thought. The journey does not end once the student has come to a greater understanding of historical truths such as the fact that the original man is the Asiatic Black man; this knowledge is simply the foundation. If the knowledge of self were limited to man's origins, it would become no more than a slogan or trite saying and would never lead the student to the greatest power and knowledge.

The knowledge of self begins with a curriculum that should be implemented in schools. The current school curriculum and pedagogy is disconnected from the reality of Black students. Freire (2000) argues that students are made to be "abstract, isolated, independent, and unattached to the world, that the world exists as a reality apart" (p. 69). This poses a major problem, as Muhammad pointed out that each of the disciplines exist within the students. He opposed the commonly held belief that our students are taking math, science, or history, positing instead that we are history, math, science, and all of the other disciplines. In understanding this, Muhammad's students are constantly seeking mastery over the self as well as educing new thoughts and ideas around each of the disciplines. The knowledge of self helps students to develop voice, which is essential in pulling forth purpose and the essence of God in the individual.

Scholars in multicultural education agree that voice is an essential component in the teaching and learning process (Gollnick & Chinn, 2006; Nieto & Bode, 2008; McLaren 2007). In fact, Gollnick and Chinn (2006) connect education with the silencing of marginalized groups:

> Most schools today legitimate only the voice of the dominant culture—the standard English and world perspective of the white middle class. Many of the students, especially those from oppressed groups, learn to be silent or disruptive, and/or they drop out, in part because their voices are not accepted as legitimate in the classroom. (p. 368)

Today's schools purposely use official knowledge as the means to have teachers teach to the test while killing the voice of creativity within students. Macedo (2000) explains, "More and more as the corporate culture exercises more control

over schools, teachers are reduced to the role of imposing 'an official truth' pre-
determined by 'a small group of people who analyze, execute, make decisions,
and run things in the political, economic and ideological system'" (p. 5). Official
knowledge is described as knowledge that the State sanctions or approves.
Banks (2008) gives an excellent illustration of official knowledge with the description of teachers' retelling of the Sacajawea and Geronimo stories in history
courses:

> Consequently, most of the ethnic groups and women added to the curriculum
> have values and roles consistent with those of the dominant culture. Men and
> women who challenged the status quo and dominant institutions are less likely
> to be selected for inclusion into the curriculum. Thus, Sacajawea is more likely
> to be chosen for inclusion than is Geronimo because she helped Whites to con-
> quer Native American lands. Geronimo resisted the takeover of Native Ameri-
> can lands by Whites. (p. 31)

Official knowledge is often used to distort reality and thus has little to no implications in its current practice for knowledge of self. Macedo (2000) again explains:

> On the contrary, our so-called democratic schools are based on an instrumental
> skills-banking approach that often prevents the development of the kind of
> thinking that enables one to "read the world" critically and to understand the
> reasons and linkages behind facts. By and large this instrumentalist approach to
> education is characterized by mindless, meaningless drills and exercises given
> "in preparation of multiple choice exams" and by teachers writing gobbledy-
> gook imitation of the psychobabble that surrounds them. As State Departments
> of Education reassert their control over the curriculum via mandated standar-
> dized tests, this form of mindless skills-based education is gaining more cur-
> rency as tests guide teaching while "learning that address[es] the relationship of
> the self to public life, social responsibility, to the broader demands of citizen-
> ship" is sidelined. (pp. 3–4)

An example of official knowledge can be seen in the difference between Malcolm X's teachings and the distorted stories typically contained in American
history books. Okafor (2006) posits, ". . . it would appear that mainstream histo-
riography portrays Malcolm as the polar opposite of Dr. Martin Luther King
through inferences and images that make Malcolm look like an apostle of violence in contrast to a peace loving and non-violence oriented King" (p. 188).
An even more contemporary example of official knowledge is the noticed absence of The Million Man March from some history texts used in schools or the
complete lack of in-depth examination of Elijah Muhammad or his ideas about
the knowledge of self.

Muhammad's ideas supersede the contemporary curriculum. The concept of
his knowledge of self develops much in the same way that a seed grows; at the
proper time and with the right ingredients, the seed will burst forth into a new
creation with the ability to reproduce itself. Muhammad's pedagogy began with

instruction in social science concepts which, if carefully studied and practiced, translated into a new culture. And as Parker (2001) notes, "Culture is learned." Ultimately, Elijah Muhammad's students began to see how the social reproduction theory had played a role in their education; it eventually impacted their everyday lives. This revelation inspired the students to seek more knowledge as the means to more fully understand and overcome the cycle of ignorance that was constructed by the culture producers.

Similar to the "White architects of Black education," who also began their educational instruction with social science concepts, Muhammad connected the social science concepts in a scientific way. Muhammad's curriculum began with concepts similar to the ten themes established by the National Council for Social Studies (NCSS), which met strong opposition among conservatives fearful of diminishing patriotism among American citizenry. The ten themes were: a) Culture; b) Time Continuity, and Change; c) People, Places and Environment; d) Individual, Development and Identity; e) Individuals, Groups, and Institutions; f) Power, Authority, Governance; g) Production, Distribution, and Consumption (e.g., What things do people in our community want that they don't really need?); h) Science, Technology and Society; i) Global connections; and j) Civic ideals and practices.

Elijah Muhammad's work can be seen in these NCSS themes: a) Culture— Elijah Muhammad raises the point of Black people in America not knowing their true names, language, or religion; b) Time, Continuity and Change— Muhammad questioned the following: What is Time? How do you calculate time? Has the Black man in American been making Time? Is the universe in a process of evolution? Are we in a process of evolution? c) People, Places and Environment—Muhammad questioned the following: What is the connection between man, earth and universe? What is the area in square miles of the planet earth? How much is land and how much is water? How much of the useful land was occupied by the original man? How much is used by the Colored man? What is the circumference of the earth? d) Individual Identity—Muhammad questioned the following: Who is the original man? Who is the colored man? How was the label *Negro* created? What is the role of education in making a slave? What psychological strategies were used to make a slave? e) Power, Authority and Governance—Muhammad questioned: How did white people come to rule the world? What was the particular reason for their rule? What is the time limit of White people's rule? How has the Black man been governed under White rule? Who has supreme power over all things? f) Production, Distribution, and Consumption—Muhammad questioned: What are Black people producing in North America? Why are Black people in America constantly asking for jobs? Do we need land of our own? Should we enter into international trade to get something that we can call our own?

These are just a few of the similarities between Elijah Muhammad's ideas and the NCSS's ten themes. The problem book, which is a key component of the early curriculum put forth by Elijah Muhammad similar to the social studies standards, provided a springboard to launch students into their quest for more knowledge. The above questions do not encompass the entire problem book, but they demonstrate that Muhammad's work was educational and that, similar to curriculum theorists, Muhammad had an organizational plan for education. Muhammad's social science concepts provided an inspiration that would ultimately lead to a much higher science of study. This is why Elijah Muhammad said, "I just want to teach you the science." In fact, his teacher, Master Fard Muhammad, gave him the specific assignment of teaching the "lost found." Regarding the significance of the knowledge of self Elijah Muhammad writes,

> It is knowledge of self that the so-called Negroes lack which keeps them from enjoying freedom, justice and equality. This belongs to them divinely as much as it does to other nations of the earth. It is Allah's will and purpose that we shall know ourselves. Therefore he came himself to teach us the knowledge of self. (p. 31)

Teaching the knowledge of self is the mission given to Elijah Muhammad by his teacher, and it is the knowledge of self that will ultimately lead Black people into a full and complete freedom. The concept is politically charged when linked to the topic of the education of Black people, because the ruling powers, realizing that it will ultimately lead to the demise of the current order, fear knowledge of self above all. In early 2007, two Los Angeles charter school teachers were fired for planning to have students celebrate Black History Month by reading a poem and laying a wreath in honor of Emmett Till. The school administrators felt the idea of examining Emmett Till was inappropriate and that Black History Month should be about celebrating positive figures (Retrieved February 25, 2009 from: http://articles.latimes.com/2007/mar/19/local/me-newcharter19).

Numerous similar cases have existed throughout the Black experience, and many teachers have been punished simply for trying to teach Black students knowledge of self. However, this is not surprising when considering that historically, Blacks were not allowed to read, write, or even think independently of their slave masters. Spring (2007) notes:

> Literacy was a punishable crime for enslaved Africans in the South. However, by the outbreak of the Civil War in 1860, it is estimated that 5 percent of slaves had learned how to read, sometimes at the risk of life or limb. Individual slaves would sneak books and teach themselves while hiding from their masters. (p. 52)

Anyone attempting to teach Blacks the knowledge of self has historically been regarded as the potential enemy of the ruling powers. Elijah Muhammad brilliantly argued, "The worst kind of crime has been committed against us, for we were robbed of our desire to even think and do for ourselves" (p. 37).

Similarly, in his passion to uplift the Black people, Carter G. Woodson proposed the study of Black history. His work met hostility from the highest levels, including the Department of Justice. Spivey (2003) notes,

The Federal Government saw the Black History Movement as a threat because it intended to enlighten and inspire blacks to work to transform American society. By 1940 there was a widening government plot against Woodson that had begun at least twenty years earlier. Woodson was the target of Attorney General A. Mitchell Palmer and the Department of Justice. (pp. 22–23)

Like Woodson, Elijah Muhammad encountered a full court press by government agents who actively sought to destroy his progress in educating Black people. But Muhammad had already predicted that anyone attempting to teach the knowledge of self to Black people would be watched and in some cases prosecuted. Spivey (2003) documents the powers that sought to deny Black people the knowledge of self:

The FBI took particular notice of books on black history, especially those that were in demand, such as works by Woodson. The United States government clandestinely plotted against black intellectuals and consciousness within the African American community . . . By the 1960s the FBI had a specialized unit, called Division Five, with the primary mission of focusing on black intellectual activists. This group worked in conjunction with COINTELPRO, the FBI's counter-intelligence program to neutralize the Civil Rights Movement and other black activist groups. (pp. 23–24)

Ultimately, those with the highest decision-making authority decided that Black people must never attain the knowledge of self. Nothing has changed dramatically since that time with regard to underlying philosophy of Black education. Black education remains tied to the economic needs of those who control the society. General Samuel Armstrong, one of the "White Architects" who influenced Black education in the South, espoused an educational doctrine of subservience that made Blacks laborers for the White ruling class (Spring, 2007; Watkins, 2001). The school curriculum was tied to a larger society in which Black people would be trained to perform better services for this class of rulers. Elijah Muhammad explained,

Since our being brought here in chains to the shores of America, our brain power, labor, skills talent and wealth have been taken, given and spent toward the building and adding to the civilization of another people. It is time for you and me, the so-called Negroes, to start doing for ourselves. (p. 56)

In order to effectively do so, Muhammad proposed the following:

We [Black people] must begin at the cradle and teach our babies that they must do for self . . . We must teach our children now with an enthusiasm exceeding that which our slave-masters used in having our forefathers imbed the seed of dependency within us. We must stop the process of giving our brain power, labor, and wealth to our slave-masters' children. We must eliminate the master-slave relationship. (p. 57)

In a revolutionary stance, Muhammad declared, "We must educate ourselves and our children into the rich power of knowledge which has elevated every people who have sought and used it" (p. 57). The key knowledge advocated by Elijah Muhammad was knowledge of self and God. Like those of yesteryear, today's Black education-centered problems are connected to a curriculum that is controlled by the White ruling powers and does not lead to true freedom.

Multicultural Education

The multicultural education movement in America was birthed as a direct result of the country's Civil Rights movement, which, while largely examined from the perspective of civil rights leaders, was enhanced by several Black leaders and their ideas about justice and equality. One of those leaders, who played a significant role in advancing the civil rights and multicultural movements, was Elijah Muhammad. Eric Lincoln, a long-time scholar on the Nation of Islam, named Elijah Muhammad as a major contributor to multicultural education, saying, "We in America can thank Mr. Muhammad for the major role he played in helping us to understand and prepare for what lies ahead in the multi-culture, where religion is so basic to human understanding and cooperation" (Muhammad, 2000, p. 6).

Believing Elijah Muhammad could never be associated with multicultural education, I was astounded upon first reading these words several years ago. According to Banks (2008), multicultural education is typically defined using an *additive approach*, in which "cultural content, concepts and themes are added to the curriculum without changing its basic structure, purposes and characteristics" (p. 47). The additive approach to multicultural education is contrasted by the notions of radical or critical multicultural theorists, who argue that multicultural education should address the issues of racism and classism (Sleeter cited in Noel 2008, McLaren, 2007). Those considered radical multicultural theorists assert that the additive approach is a "too watered down" or a "feel good" approach, and thus lacks the substance needed to change the horrendous conditions of inequality that exist in schools and in the larger society.

In one of his lectures, Minister Farrakhan disclosed the multicultural dimension of the Nation of Islam when he proposed that Wallace Fard Muhammad came to save White people. Indeed, the multicultural education movement, when examined properly, is beneficial to people of European descent; it gives them the ability to self-reflect and view the world from the other perspectives. More importantly, multicultural education is about the destruction of mythical history that distorts and hides the truth. It is an exploder of myths (Kincheloe and Steinberg, 1997). Strands of Elijah Muhammad's teachings can be seen woven throughout the fabric of multicultural education.

James Banks (2008), who is considered the founder of the multicultural education movement, has pointed out that multicultural education is a reform effort centered on the idea of equality. Banks highlights, "It grew out of the civil rights movement grounded in Western democratic ideals such as freedom, justice, and equality" (p. 9). One could argue that freedom, justice, and equality are not Western ideals but are founded in the very principles of life. According to Elijah Muhammad, the notions of freedom, justice, and equality were rooted in the makeup of the Universe; in order to really observe these principles at work, one simply has to look at the signs—the sun, moon, and stars—that exist in the heavens. The sun represents freedom, as it gives light, energy, and life freely to all people. The moon represents equality, in that it balances the water from overtaking the land. And the stars represent justice in that each of us is justified in our existence. To illustrate his point, Muhammad used the example of the star-shaped badge worn by law enforcement officials who rightfully administer justice.

Elijah Muhammad argued that Blacks wanted freedom, justice, equality, and independence. Muhammad's ideas, while similar to Banks,' go much deeper into universal laws that must be understood in order to develop an effective educational system that would provide freedom, justice, equality, and independence. One must first determine how to create an educational system that aligns with the universal principles espoused by Elijah Muhammad. Such a system would require the sun to represent the gifts and talents that each individual provides humanity freely, the moon to represent an education that would help us to find balance in life, and the stars to represent education that helps us to justify our purpose for existence. This new conception would in turn require us to rethink our concept of society, education, and school.

The first step in changing our thinking about society, education, and school is to require instruction that does not sugarcoat the historical racism and inequality that serve as the foundation for American life. Most American students have been taught a mythical history of the United States that serves the purpose of maintaining White supremacy and world hegemony. It is quite amazing to attend all-White schools and witness how White students view other cultures as being savage and inferior. Responsibility for this view lies partly with the teachers and textbooks that have been Europeanized to support White supremacy. This has had a deleterious effect on the non-White masses. For some Blacks, it has led to a mindset that the ultimate goal is to be as White as possible with regard to behavior and thinking. However, despite best efforts to become White by some people of so-called "color," full access to White privilege has still been denied. Banks (2008) explains this phenomenon: "Some individuals of color, such as many African Americans, Native Americans, and Puerto Rican Americans, in their effort to assimilate and participate fully in mainstream institutions, become very Anglo Saxon in their ways of viewing the world and in their values and behavior" (p. 3). The educational system should be credited for this type of thinking, as it was a part of the ideology used to teach Native Americans: "kill the Indian and keep the man." Thus, the multicultural education movement as an exploder of myths would have to

. . . advocate that the truth about the West should be told, that its debt to people
of color and women be recognized and included in the curriculum and the dis-
crepancies between the ideals of freedom and equality, and the realities of racism and sexism, be taught to students. (Banks, 2008, p. 6)

Like many before him, Elijah Muhammad attacked the White supremacist mythology taught to the masses; however, like none before him, Muhammad
shocked the world when he pronounced "the whiteman [sic] is the devil." Ultimately, what Muhammad was doing went beyond the multicultural education
movement into the origin of Whiteness. While some Whites were extolling their
Standard of beauty—previously the only culturally acceptable model, Elijah
Muhammad was saying, "Black is beautiful; the White Standard is the devil."
This forced Whites to reexamine their Standard with the lenses of equality and
freedom in comparison to the darker skin peoples of the earth; suddenly, the
White Standard was not necessarily the most beautiful. Thus, the mind of White
supremacy was attacked with a force and power more than equal to the thought
that brought White supremacy into existence. The masses could not accept this
exegesis of Whiteness, having been indoctrinated to see Whites as superior. A
key goal of Elijah Muhammad's teaching was to give Whites another perspective, but more importantly, to give Black people a way of deconstructing the
White mind that had been placed in them that made some Blacks view the world
with a Eurocentric perspective. This type of teaching would also break the mind
of White supremacy so thoroughly engrained in White people. As one of my
students pointed out, multicultural education is really for White students.

Banks (2008) explains, "A key goal of multicultural education is to help individuals gain greater self-understanding by viewing themselves from the perspective of other cultures" (p. 2). This certainly applies to White students, as they
are afforded what Howard (2006) calls the "luxury of ignorance." Howard notes,
"Individuals from the dominant group are usually unaware of their own power
and can carry on the daily activities of their lives without any substantial knowledge about, or meaningful interaction with, those people who are not a part of
the dominant group" (p. 61). Howard explains that this luxury is not afforded to
other groups whose "lives demand expertise in translation and transition between their own culture and the culture of dominance" (p. 62). Multicultural
education opens the door for the destruction of the mis-education of the masses
by teaching multiple perspectives of the world that move beyond the Euro-
centered view.

Today, scholars openly talk about Whiteness; much of the credit for this belongs to Elijah Muhammad's teachings. In talking about racism, Peter McLaren
(2007) highlights the following:

The specific struggle that I wish to address is that of choosing against whiteness. Yet is it possible for us to choose against whiteness given that, historically, the practice of whiteness has brought about such a devastating denial, disas-
sembly, and destruction of other races? One would think that such a choice
against whiteness would be morally self evident. However, precisely because

whiteness is so pervasive it remains difficult to identify, to challenge, and to separate from our daily lives. My message is that we must create a new public sphere where the practice of whiteness is not only identified and analyzed but also contested and destroyed. For choosing against whiteness is the hope and promise of the future. (p. 261)

The hope for the destruction of Whiteness (not White people) and the creation of the New World lies in the ideas espoused by Elijah Muhammad. McLaren (2007) highlights that in moments of despair, movements such as The Million Man March offer a possibility of hope. The Million Man March was a powerful sign of the presence of Muhammad's revolutionary education endeavor. The Million Man March demonstrates what Shor and Freire (1987) calls an educational endeavor that should be examined as "liberating education." Freire argues, "But there is another place for the existence of and the development of liberating education which is precisely in the intimacy of social movements" (p. 38). The Million Man March has had a deep impact on life in America. Schools and school systems have purposely limited discussion of this movement. Unknown to most is the role that Elijah Muhammad played in planting the thought for The Million Man March in Minister Farrakhan, its convener.

The Million Man March has evolved into what is now called the Millions More Movement and has nine ministries that are designed to connect educated Black America to the masses. One of the ministries, the ministry of education, drives all of the others. I envision the nine ministries as the foundation for schools or colleges within a future New University. The birth of these schools, colleges, and universities will usher in a New World. Elijah Muhammad's work and mission is still alive and having an impact, playing a role in every aspect of American and international life. Muhammad's life mission demonstrates the profound love necessary to teach, especially to teach a people who have been indoctrinated to be subservient through years of mis-education. Elijah Muhammad has indeed won and the truth of his pronouncements can be seen in the events we are currently experiencing at home and abroad.

Critical Pedagogy

McLaren (2007) notes that critical pedagogy is "fundamentally concerned with understanding the relationship between power and knowledge" (p. 209). Critical understanding of the relationship between power and knowledge is essential for Black people who have been dominated by European education.

A careful study of the educational experiences of Black people in America demonstrates that education was in fact mis-education. The American education process was specifically designed for the purpose of making slaves. This mis-educational process was designed to make Blacks servants of those who held dominant positions. In his book, *Message to the Blackman in America,* Muhammad (1965) quotes Edwin Embree:

We have as far as possible, closed every avenue by which light may enter the slaves mind. If we could extinguish the capacity to see the light, our work would be complete; they would be on a level with the beast of the field and we should be safe. (p. 186)

Embree's light mentioned here represents knowledge. The cutting or depriving of knowledge was a prerequisite for maintaining White rule over Black people. Watkins (2001) notes how White philanthropists scripted Black education for seventy-five years after the Civil War:

From the onset the white architects of black education understood the power of ideas. They carefully selected and sponsored knowledge, which contributed to obedience, subservience, and political docility . . . Colonial education had to be fitted to the American south. This undertaking required the efforts of both the ideologists and the financers. Corporate philanthropists joined forces with racial sociologist to design seventy five years of education for blacks. (pp. 41–42)

Elijah Muhammad, knowing the importance of knowledge and proper education, challenged the foundation of the White supremacist construction of Black education. This challenge in educational terms is called *critical pedagogy* and is the junction at which the relationship between power and knowledge is examined. Elijah Muhammad raised several points related to critical educational theory, but more importantly, he provided knowledge to overcome the curriculum prescribed by those who rule. Muhammad raised the following points regarding power and knowledge:

Certainly the so-called Negroes are being schooled, but is this education the equal of that of their slave masters? No; the so called Negroes are still begging for equal education. After blinding them to the knowledge of self and their own kind for 400 years, the slave masters refuse to civilize the so-called Negroes into the knowledge of themselves of which they were robbed. The slave-masters also persecute and hinder anyone who tries to perform this rightful duty. (Muhammad, 1965, pp. 44–45)

Muhammad brilliantly points out that the "so-called Negro" is being "schooled" but not educated. In his book, *Too Much Schooling and Too Little Education,* Shujaa (1994) distinguishes the difference between education and schooling. Shujaa explains the process of schooling, in which Black students are taught to fit into the dominant society, versus the process of education, in which students are taught to understand their potential. Therefore, Muhammad is correct when he says that Blacks are being schooled as opposed to being educated. The schooling process of Black people in America is not educing the genetic power that lies dormant within the individual because the schooling process put to death the creative power of self. Asante (2005) asserts that he has never "found a school in the United States run by Whites that adequately prepares Black children to enter the world as sane human beings" (p. 65). Freire (2000) believes this version of education actually turns Blacks into "beings for others," which can be interpreted to mean that the oppressed are schooled in the interests of those who oppress them. Woodson (1999) concurs:

> When you control a man's thinking you do not have to worry about his actions. You do not have to tell him stand here or go yonder. He will find his proper place and will stay in it. You do not need to send him to the back door. He will go without being told. In fact, if there is no back door he will cut one for his special benefit. His education makes it necessary. (p. xii)

The mis-education of African American children can be seen in visiting what are called "inner-city" schools and communities. These institutions represent what is manifest to the eye as social decay. Upon closer examination, it is apparent this mis-education is not limited to the inner city; it can be also viewed as a reflection of what is taking place in the minds of those who rule. Elijah Muhammad (1965) raised the issue of power and knowledge throughout his teaching, pointing out:

> You must know that you have not been rightly civilized. No one can enslave another who has equal knowledge. My people lack science of the right kind. Allah is here to give you and me superior knowledge of things and a country to ourselves. Separation of the so-called Negroes from their slave masters is a must. (p. 45)

In this statement Muhammad raises issue with contemporary education and civilization. The educational system, having been designed by those interested in maintaining White supremacy, is an excellent reference for the question of how some minority populations have been improperly civilized and denied access to equal knowledge. The system does not give those populations the education needed to be free peoples. Muhammad (1965) discusses the 1920s debate over Black education and the type of education that would have actually been necessary for Blacks to have been declared free:

> I recall, in 1922 or 1923, when a debate was taking place in Congress concerning appropriation of funds for Howard University, a school set aside to train my people, in the nation's capital. A senator said this, and it is in the records to be examined in effect: What would be the need of the government appropriating money to educate Negroes? He said that they would not teach our people the science of modern warfare (defense), birth control or chemistry. He knew these were things free people must know in order to protect, preserve, and advance themselves. We have not been able to protect, preserve and advance ourselves. This shows the slave-master has been very successful in dominating us with an education beneficial to him. (p. 40)

Today, nothing has changed; in fact, schools have become more equipped to perform this function of domination. The *No Child Left Behind Act of 2001* (NCLB) is evidence of this dominating function of education that has been beneficial to the world shapers. NCLB mandates exams that have made schools more oppressive for students who are not White or upper class, resulting in what some have called *being black in school*—the intentional targeting or removal of some Black children in order to raise the overall test scores of a particular school. Ultimately, we must question who has made and continues to make decisions regarding the education of Black children. Have these decision makers been Whites in positions of power? The answer is a resounding "Yes!" and validates the argument of Elijah Muhammad and Carter G. Woodson that the education of Black people is left completely in the hands of those who have enslaved them.

Indeed, Muhammad and Woodson correctly described the power relation that exists in schools today. Muhammad (1965) notes, "Today with all of our white civilized schooling, we have not been taught our own. They will never teach us of our own" (p. 48). Woodson (1999) concurs: "Negroes have NO CONTROL of their education and have little voice in their other affairs pertaining thereto" (p. 22). Our nation's educational history has only proven them right. One school board in Lafayette, Louisiana, voted 7–2 against incorporating Black history in district schools. This is just one example of the continued White dominance of Black education.

The disastrous results of standardized testing as the right arm of White supremacist education have caused educational scholars to ponder what is needed to create the best educational program for all children and have resulted in a number of studies related to closing the achievement gap between Black and White students in particular. Scholars and educators who are concerned with issues of social justice and educational equality have brilliantly identified problems with the education of non-White students. Problems such as racism, inequitable school funding, the lack of diversity in a Euro-centered curriculum, biased standardized tests, and a majority White teaching force are some factors that contribute to the so-called gap. However, a major part of the problem in Black education also lies in what Woodson called 'education outside of the control of Black people.' Woodson (1999) eloquently stated, "The education of the Negroes, then, the most important thing in the uplift of the Negroes, is almost entirely in the hands of those who enslaved them and now segregate them" (p. 22). Even in cases where Blacks seem to be in control of the educational system, they are often educated to maintain or oversee public schools—the modern plantation. Woodson (1999) accurately describes this problem,

> With mis-educated Negroes in control themselves, however, it is doubtful that the system would be very much different from what it is or that it would rapidly undergo change. The Negroes thus placed in charge would be the products of the same system and would show more conception of the task at hand than do the whites who have educated them and shaped their minds as they would have them function. (p. 23)

Woodson's description of the complexity of Black education is even more applicable today than at the time of its writing. In fact, the new standardization of education has resulted in lack of vision about approaching the problems of Black education. Too many schools have continued to use European philosophy as the basis for all education and Black teachers, while realizing something is wrong with the educational system, have not been able to accurately pinpoint the problem:

> Negro educators of today may have more sympathy and interest in the race than the Whites now exploiting Negro institutions as educators, but the former have no more vision than their competitors. Taught from the same books of the same bias, trained by Caucasians of the same prejudices or by Negroes of enslaved minds, one generation of Negro teachers after another has served for no higher purpose than to do what they are told to do. In other words, a Negro teacher instructing Negro children is in many respects a White teacher thus engaged, for the program in each case is about the same. (Woodson, 1999, p. 23)

This should raise a question of what type of education is needed to begin the education of Black people in America and eventually, the human family. What curriculum must be set up to ignite the spark in people's minds? Woodson (1999) argues, "Real education means to inspire people to live more abundantly, to learn to begin life as they find it and make it better, but the instruction so far given Negroes in colleges and universities has worked to the contrary" (p. 29). Elijah Muhammad (1965), a man who completed school only through the fourth grade, argued, "Knowledge is the result of learning and is a force or energy that makes its bearer accomplish or overcome obstacles, barriers and resistance" (p. 41).

Separate Schools

Elijah Muhammad (1965) raised the question of separating Black children from Whites during their early school years. He believed that Black children's early years should be marked by attendance in schools comprised completely of other Black students, conscious teachers, and a curriculum centered around, the knowledge of self:

> Education for my people should be where our children are off to themselves for the first 15 or 16 years in classes separated by sex. Then they could and should seek higher education without the danger of losing respect for self or seeking to lose their identity. No people strive to lose themselves among other people except the so-called American Negro. This they do because of their lack of knowledge of self. (p. 39)

Some coined this concept as *Black separatism,* which has been viewed as extreme and radical. Most people are afraid to mention separation in schools, but Elijah Muhammad clearly understood its deeper meaning. For him there was a difference between *separation* and *segregation*; additionally, Muhammad was likely considering the psychological impact of White supremacy and racism on the American society. He foresaw that forcing Black children to attend majority

White schools without deconstructing the White supremacist curriculum would prove fatal to Black identity. Instead, Muhammad expressed that separation was important in the early grades because Black children needed a foundation rooted in themselves. For example, he explains, "We know that kindergarten children and first graders, once in Islam, cannot be taken into Christian schools without having to suffer mockery and attack from the Christian children and from the Christian teachers who hate Islam, the God of Islam, and the Prophets of Islam" (p. 214). Asante (2005) further contends that a rejection of one's heritage can result in *menticide*, and concluded that Black people must reject "European America as absolute teacher."

Interestingly, although Muhammad was cast as a reverse racist and a Black separatist for his teachings, the reality is that a majority of schools are more separate today than they were 50 years ago, before the *Brown v. Board of Education* decision. The integration of schools has resulted in student tracking programs such as those identifying the gifted and talented. These programs, while housed on majority Black campuses, will sometimes have majority White students, and the teaching methodology and privileges for students in these programs is completely different from what is given to students placed in regular classrooms. Nieto and Bode (2008) explain the negative impact of tracking:

> Tracking leaves its mark on pedagogy as well. Students in the lowest levels, for example, are the most likely students to be subjected to rote memorization and worn methods, as their teachers often feel these are the children who most need to master the basics. (p. 94)

Ultimately, what happens in many cases is the creation of schools within the school. The school-within-a-school construct reinforces the mentality of White supremacy and Black inferiority; in most cases, the gifted classes are made up of White students, whereas Black students are placed in regular classes or special education. Oakes (1985), in a study of tracking programs, found that tracking tended to be based on ideas that maintain class and race privilege. The question of separation must therefore be examined from Muhammad's perspective with more depth and analysis.

What did Muhammad mean by separation? Freire (2000) is a very common focus of study for critical educational theorists, but he has never been mentioned as being a separatist despite the similarity of his ideas to Elijah Muhammad's educational philosophy:

> The truth is, however, that the oppressed are not "marginals"; are not people living "outside" society. They have always been "inside"—inside the structure so that they can become "beings for others." The solution is not to integrate them into the structure of oppression, but to transform that structure so that they can become "beings for themselves". (p. 74)

Freire's analysis provides a very powerful way of examining why mental separation is a necessity. Elijah Muhammad (1965) explains the reason behind the call for separate education and the creation of a new society that would make Black people "beings for themselves":

> My people should get an education which will benefit their own people and not an education adding to the "storehouse" of their teacher. We need education, but an education which removes from us the shackles of slavery and servitude. Get an education, but not an education which leaves us in an inferior position and without a future. Get an education, but not an education that leaves us looking to the slave-master for a job. (p. 39)

While Muhammad's ideas seemed radical at the time, they were similar to the concept that has been termed *critical education*. Elijah Muhammad insisted that in order for Black people to truly be free, separation of education in the early childhood years was a necessity, considèring the Euro-centered curriculum. As Freire contended, it is because the oppressed have never been outside the structure, they have not been able to experience true freedom. Muhammad (1965) explained:

> You and I, here in America, are licking the boots of the slave-master, begging him for the right of independent people. Yes, we are licking his boots. Sir let me shine your shoes? You have been doing that for approximately 400 years. Today, if one rises up in your midst and says, "We should not lick the slave-master's boots, we should lick our own boots," you would say, He should be killed! He should be killed because he is teaching us to hate. (p. 36)

The boot illustration is evidence of the need for Black people to have an educational system that is controlled by awakened people. Muhammad (1965) stressed, "Get an education, but one which will instill the idea and desire to get something of your own, a country of your own and jobs of your own" (p. 40). This does not mean that Muhammad envisioned a school separated simply by color; he meant that a world had to be created that was totally opposite of the system of thought that created inequality, suffering, oppression, and death. A world of love had to be created, and this world could only come about through separating completely from the mind of White supremacy that had been implanted in the masses so deeply that one major problem confronting some Blacks is that they are in fact White supremacist in their thinking. While critical educational theorists have done an excellent job describing the relationship between power and knowledge, Muhammad rocked the foundations of the educational world by summing up the power and knowledge relationship: "The slave-master will not teach you the knowledge of self, as there would not be a master-slave relationship any longer" (p. 37).

Critical Race Theory and White Studies

Critical race theory and critical White studies are two fields that have emerged to inform our understanding of education. Critical race theory is primarily concerned with race and its impact on American life. Ladson-Billings (2003) notes this origin of critical race theory: "Critical race theory sprang up in the mid-1970s with the early work of legal scholar Derrick Bell and Alan Freeman, both of whom were distressed over the slow pace of racial reform in the United States" (p. 8). Critical race theory considers racism to be a normal part of American life; more importantly, critical race theorists seek to expose racism and its impact on American life.

The impact of race and racism is clearly seen in the educational arena. Muhammad (1965) taught that the first Blacks brought to America around 1555 were made slaves and that through an educational process Black people were made blind, deaf, and dumb. The process of dehumanization took 64 years, in which the newly arrived people were completely robbed of the knowledge of self. Lynch explains how this process involved the dehumanization of the newly arrived peoples: "Hence both the horse and the nigger must be broken; that is, break them from one form of mental life to another—keep the body and take the mind" (Hassan-El, 1999, p.14). The process of dehumanization through White supremacy resulted in a society that was thoroughly ingrained with the ideology of racism at the core. In order to justify the mistreatment of human beings, the rulers of the country had to include institutions, ideologies, and theories that supported racism. As a result, racism became a natural part of the American landscape. Through skillful manipulation, the masses of White people were blinded to inequalities that existed and still exist today. Howard (2006) termed this the *luxury of ignorance* that has continued to impact the society: "Appleby likens the luxury of ignorance to a deep forgetting that has clouded White awareness of the realities of history" (p. 63). This luxury of ignorance provides Whites with the privilege of not knowing the historical reality of oppression and the role of racism and its impact on darker-skinned people. Ignoring these issues or remaining ignorant leads some White people to believe in the existence of a color-blind society while never realizing that the fundamental idea of racism was built into the institutions that were supposedly providing freedom and justice for all people.

In the schools, children are never taught to critically analyze the concepts of freedom and justice from multiple perspectives; in fact, Black children are educated to believe they live in a country that strives for democracy and freedom for all people. This is part of the ultimate brainwash, because in some places in the South, Blacks have only been "free" to exercise their right to vote for fewer than 50 years. Today, neither Black students nor White students understand the historical inequities that have shaped the current times.

This has resulted in educational institutions that providing an "official story" that omits the inequalities that exist in the larger society. Pinar (2004) explains, "The official story a nation or culture tells itself—often evident in school curriculum hides other truths. What we as a nation try not to remember—genocide, slavery, lynching, prison rape—structures the politics of our collective identification and imagined affiliation." (p. 38)

Another place that this virulent racism has been practiced and taught has been in religion. Banks (1996) discusses the role of Christianity in perpetuating racism:

> As the Christian European nations conquered and colonized native peoples in Africa, Asia, Australia, and the Americas-and especially as slavery developed in the Americas-the Europeans needed an ideology that was consistent with both their Christian beliefs and the colonization of the native peoples of these lands. Racism developed as an ideology to meet both needs. (p. 67)

Elijah Muhammad attacked both of the institutions responsible for mis-educating the masses. When he referred to Christianity as "a slave-making religion," he offended many of us who were Christians. In essence, however, Muhammad was forcing us to examine how knowledge is constructed by those in dominant positions. Howard (2006) points out, "Christian notions of dominion, choseness, singularity of truth and divine sanction of temporal patriarchal authority were well suited to the task of justifying slavery, land theft, and other forms of White supremacy" (p. 60). This ideology was and is at the core of American education. In describing the role of Christianity in reinforcing White supremacy, Elijah Muhammad was breaking from the early foundations of education, which were based on European theological justification for White rule. This did not make Muhammad a reverse racist because his teachings were based on truths that had been hidden or were unknown to the masses but had been taught to him by Wallace D. Fard Muhammad.

Elijah Muhammad's word selection caused a shock resulting in a critical self-reflection among White people. When Muhammad said that the White man was the devil, both Blacks and Whites were astonished and angered. And in his documentary, *The Hate That Hate Produced*, Mike Wallace gave a false impression of Elijah Muhammad's teaching that has continued to blind people to what Elijah Muhammad actually intended. However, upon closer study one can see Elijah Muhammad's ideas in critical race theory and critical White studies.

The examination of critical race theory has led to what is called *White studies*. The central tenet of White studies is a reading of history in which the very concept of race is said to have been created by a White power structure in order to justify discrimination against non-Whites. Advocates of White studies argue that Whites do not see their own Whiteness racially, but regard race as something that "others" have; by emphasizing "Whiteness," they seek to change White people's view of their own racial identity. Major areas of research include the nature of White identity and privilege, the historical process by which a White racial identity was created, the relation of culture to White identity, and possible processes of social change in White identity. White studies or critical White studies examine Whiteness in relationship to racism and power.

It is possible that both critical race theory and critical White studies were influenced by Elijah Muhammad, who pointed out the root of racism, forcing White people to examine Whiteness. In fact, those in critical race theory and critical White studies would do well to reexamine Elijah Muhammad's ideas to answer questions surrounding racism and White identity.

Unlike the theorists who were trying to figure out how to uproot racism and White supremacy, Muhammad had a much deeper and more significant answer to the construct of racism. His exegesis, which shattered the prevailing scientific theories of the day used to support racism, was based on the following questions: What is the origin of racism and whiteness? Will the issue of race always exist? What was the purpose of White rule?

Muhammad pointed out that the origin of racism and Whiteness was a Black scientist named Yakub who, at the age of six, discovered that opposites attract and determined that one day he would make a man that would be opposite of the Black man. This man would be given the wisdom and knowledge to rule the Black man until one was produced with a greater knowledge:

> This man, Yakub, discovered in the germ of the black man, that he had two people in him, and learned through study and experimenting on the germ that this second germ could produce a powerful people that would be able to rule that which they came from. They would be able to rule for around six thousand years or until the father of the aboriginal produced one superior to his man. He had taken, through experimental work on the germ of man, a people of what we call today a white race, but before he produced the white race, he produced a brown race, then he produced a yellow race and so on. (Muhammad, 1993, p. 6)

According to Muhammad this process of grafting included creating an environment that produced in the White man a nature predicated on deception, lies, and murder:

> Yes after Mr. Yakub making the man, white from black, then the question is how yet did he become evil? This was done through the grafting, too. In the grafting of the child, of the white out of black, he taught nurses that as soon as the baby comes to birth, if it is a black baby, then give it over to the cremators or to some wild beast: destroy that child. If the mother is not looking at the child or watching you too closely, nurse, take a needle, a sharp needle, and prick it in the brain of the baby and tell the mother that her child was still-born; we call them dead under that name still-born. This process went on throughout the brown child for another browner one. If that lesser brown was killed the browner was saved, the lighter one, or we say the lighter was saved all throughout. By having this murder inserted into the mind of the nurses to destroy the darker or the browner or the yellow, until they got the white one, once the white one came in, naturally this was in the nature of the white one: to then object to anything other than the white as a human being: consequently, he would try to destroy or kill anything that is coming into his race. (Muhammad, 1993, p. 11–12)

According to Muhammad, "This made it easy to teach the man a wisdom contrary and opposed to the wisdom of right because Yakub's man was not after producing a man that was of the same or would think the same, like the one he was taken from" (Muhammad, 1993, p. 11). The education of Yakub's man provided him with the necessary knowledge to rule Black people until one with a greater knowledge would be born. Clearly, studying Muhammad's revelation about the origin of the White man gives answer to the question of the root existence of racism.

If by nature the White man was created to rule the Black man, by what process would White man set up his rule? Would racism be at the very root of his ability to rule? By creating a world that at its very base is rooted in racism, White people could justify the denial of equality, freedom, and justice to those different from them. It would also mean that to undo racism, we would have to think like Yakub, who began with a thought and from that thought made a reality. So to break racism, we must get at the thought. But there is more. It was the thought of producing a man able to rule the darker-skinned peoples in addition to the process of killing the Black child that ultimately led to the inclination to set up a world rooted in racism. Ultimately, to destroy the mind of racism there must be a greater knowledge than the knowledge that introduced the concept of racism.

This is very interesting, as the real battle actually seems to be about whose knowledge will rule. Those wishing to maintain White supremacy would be fearful of any knowledge that would free humanity from the disease of racism, as this would mean the destruction of Whiteness, with implications for issues of equality and justice. I wonder if this process of grafting could also have implications in addressing the real problem of education facing students of so-called color today. Is it possible that teachers are unknowingly playing a role similar to the nurses in Yakub's time, pricking the brains of Black children by denying them knowledge of self, thus resulting in too many still births?

The ideology of education in America is at its root based on White philosophers who never considered Black people as human. This lack of understanding about or interest in enlightening Black people could imply that a majority of the educational theorists and their philosophies would be insufficient in developing the potential in Black children. It could also be that ultimately, some of these teaching strategies and educational philosophies are about killing those children that have dispositions aligned with original Black thought.

While some thought the concept of integration simply meant Blacks sitting next to Whites in the classroom, Muhammad had a much deeper analysis. In an interview (Muhammad, 1993), Muhammad posited that skin color is not the problem—Blacks and Whites could live alongside each other. According to Muhammad, the problem moves beyond skin color to the actual thought and environment that brought Whiteness into existence. Muhammad (1993) notes: "This is the main thing. Not that we hate one another's color; the color could be peaceful to us, we have all kinds of colors in the universe to look at; but it is the nature or characteristic of us that we hate, that's the thing" (p. 18). Critical race theory and critical White studies are theories that correctly address major issues in the education of students. However, Elijah Muhammad's ideas on critical White studies go to the root origin of "White supremacist thought."

Muhammad's mission was completely educational, and has sparked revolutionary thinking about education and schooling.

Chapter 4

Interdisciplinary Scope

In this chapter I examine the interdisciplinary scope of the teachings of Elijah Muhammad. In every field of study the exemplary student can find relative knowledge espoused by Elijah Muhammad. Highlighted in this chapter are ideas related to the *Philosophical; Teachings on Education: critical pedagogy, critical race theory, critical white studies; Social Sciences; Sciences; math; religious studies; Women's Studies; Automobiles; Architecture; Banking; Agriculture; Islamic Studies; Language; Health; aviation.* Additionally, the chapter lays a foundation for understanding Elijah Muhammad's ideas for curriculum development in K-12 schools and higher education programs that prepare teachers.

The chapter is composed of exact quotes to help the reader develop a greater understanding of how Muhammad's work was interdisciplinary. The chapter provides a foundation for Elijah Muhammad Scholars to comparatively analyze their respective disciplines or fields of study with the teachings of Elijah Muhammad. The chapter also provides insight for those interested in developing a new school curriculum. The new curriculum will hopefully coincide with the definition espoused by Tynnetta Muhammad. Tynnetta Muhammad posits the deeper meaning of curriculum and its significance, "In this word, you have 'cur' or 'cure' and 'culum' or 'qalam' which is the Arabic word for pen. Also you have 'alam' which is the Arabic word for knowledge. Hence, curriculum is supposed to cure the mental, moral and spiritual diseases in man which result from the lack of knowledge, and pen originally was used, of course, to write curriculum" (Cited in Muhammad, 2005, p. 59). Additionally, Minister Louis Farrakhan the National Representative of Elijah Muhammad and leader of the Nation of Islam has produced several works related to education. Minister Farrakhan in his lectures, writings, and interviews clearly lays the foundation for understanding the universal aspects of Elijah Muhammad's teachings. There are five major works that I have been able to identify that epitomize Minister Farrakhan's exegesis of Elijah Muhammad's teachings as it relates to the field of education. In 1993, Minister Farrakhan published *A Torch Light for America* this significant book has implications for the totality of universal expression in the 21st century. He specifically addresses education in a chapter titled: *Fixing the Public School System.* The chapter starts by citing the inadequacy of the public school system in preparing functional citizens. Minister Farrakhan specifically points out the importance of a new educational system: "If America is unwilling to destroy the old system of education in order to create a new system of education, then America's status as a world power will quickly fade away in generation or so" (p. 46). In the same chapter, he provides what is one of the most significant philosophical writings on the purpose of education. The section highlights that "true education cultivates the person—mind, body and spirit—by bringing us closer to fulfilling our purpose for being, which is to reflect the creator" (p. 47). The chapter has several significant topics some which include the knowledge of self, putting God first, creating school safety, and honoring the teaching profession. A careful study of this chapter can provide students of education with an abundance of ideas for creating a new and better educational system.

Minister Farrakhan's *Education is the Key* is an important book that should be read by all students of education. This book is thirty pages in length. It lays the foundation for understanding the purpose of education. The nine sections in this booklet provide the necessities of spiritual education. Minister Farrakhan in the chapter *Knowledge Beyond Books* specifically points out that education is intrinsic to the human being. He (2006) argues that, "when we were birthed into the world we are birthed into a Book, a pure book; a Book that is all Truth . . . and everything around us is truth and everything around us is a book" (p. 16). This is a very powerful statement that if broken into smaller pieces could help educational scholars and students rethink the purpose of education.

In 2008, Minister Farrakhan convened a conference for educators in the Nation of Islam. The effort was designed to build a curriculum that could be adopted by the Muhammad University of Islam, universities across the nation, and the world. The initial efforts led to another education conference where Minister Farrakhan was the keynote speaker. His lecture was titled: *The Education Challenge: A New Paradigm for the 21st Century*. This was the most powerful exegesis of education that I have ever heard. The lecture, like Minister Farrakhan's other works, was deeply spiritual and foundational. Minister Farrakhan examines education as a divine act illuminating that the mission of the Christ is educational.

Another significant work by Minister Farrakhan was a lecture delivered at *The Challenging the Genius Conference* in September of 2005. At this conference Minister Farrakhan gave a message titled: *Message to the Black Educators*. The lecture provided guidance for Black educators and the significant role they play in the uplift of Black people and all of humanity. Two major themes stood out in the lecture: excellence and the origin of creation. There is a certain section in the lecture where he alludes to the teachings of Elijah Muhammad and his ideas about education. The tape should be studied particularly by those interested in the universal principles of education.

In 2006, Jabril Muhammad and Minister Farrakhan released a book titled, *Closing the Gap*. The book is loaded with ideas for the interdisciplinary scope of Elijah Muhammad's work. In the book, there are several sections that specifically deal with education. The book answers questions related to William Doll's post modern new science and curriculum. One will find the section on chaos and order one of the most powerful scientific and educational arguments related to the roles of chaos and order in the creation of the universe. *Closing the Gap* also highlights the student-teacher relationship. Minister Farrakhan delves into the attitude needed by the student in order to grow under the guidance of a master teacher. What is striking about the book is that it covers almost every imaginable discussion about the role of education. For example Michael Apple (2004) in his book *Ideology and Curriculum* refers to the role of school in making children acquiesce to the role of workers. Apple notes how kindergarten children are skillfully manipulated to give up the meaning of play for work. Apple (2004) writes, "Information which the children said they learned in school were all things that the teacher had told them during activities they called work . . . First, work includes any and all teacher-directed activities; only free-time activities were called "play" by the children" (p. 52). Minister Farrakhan in *Closing the Gap* answers the question related to fun in a profound way that catapults the role of education. Minister Farrakhan writes:

> Fun is developing the creative mind that is seen in the sperm that has intelligence to seek the egg. A light of itself in a cell that rotates and revolves in the darkness of the womb that develops that which allows it to cling to the walls of the uterus on finding a firm resting place for growth that the body will not be able to expel this strange new life within itself.

> There's intelligence there that must be fed; it must be cultivated. So the child comes into the world, nobody teaches it to coo; to say thank you. Nobody teaches it to crawl. Nobody teaches it to pull up. Nobody from the outside teaches it to walk. All of this is within itself.

> What is fun? Fun is us watching intelligence develop. Fun is feeding intelligence to create the creative mind that the child will be able to say like God, 'Be' and it is. That's fun! (p. 374)

This statement compels educators to reexamine the role of education and provides profound insight into curriculum development and curriculum theory. The concept of fun as developing the creative mind means that schooling and curriculum must move beyond regurgitation, rote memory, and standardized testing to one that cultivates creative thinking.

Minister Farrakhan's work on education is significant because it moves the student from the technical aspect of education to a more purposeful reason regarding the purpose of education. His work is foundational for building ideas for the post-modern education that scholars so often refer to as the beginning of something new. Education is a divine act and the teaching profession is one of the greatest roles that one could undertake. Education as a divine act is clearly pronounced through all of the Minister Farrakhan's work on education. One can glean from Minister Farrakhan's work the higher purpose for being an educator.

It is hopeful that the reader can glean vital aspects from this section to begin the process of *curing* the mental, moral, and spiritual diseases that afflict the whole of humanity. A note to the reader, the exact quotes listed under the section headings are not confined to a specific discipline or field of study, in fact most of the quotes have implications for a variety of disciplines.

Beyond the Philosophical

We have never known where He Himself began or who was first, God or the universe? Just who is God? What is he? Is he the essence of this universe or some invisible power, spirit, or force that has no equal comparison in his creation?

The knowledge of God has been kept a secret by twelve men on our planet for many thousands of years. The twelve pass their knowledge on from son to son, but the number possessing this knowledge is never more than twelve; and they are not to ever reveal it.

The wisest scientists have worked, studied, and search all their life long for the actual knowledge of God and have failed to obtain it. Finally, they formed their own opinions of God.

Teachings on Education

It is knowledge of self that the so-called Negroes lack which keeps them from enjoying freedom, justice, and equality. This belongs to them divinely as much as it does to other nations of the earth.

We should acquire and education where our people will become better students than their teachers. Get an education which will make our people produce jobs for self and will make our people willing and able to do for self.

Get an education, but one which will instill the idea and desire to get something of your own, a country of your own and jobs of your own.

I want an education for my people that will let them exercise the right of freedom. We are 100 years up from slavery. We are constantly being told that we are free. Why can't we take advantage of that freedom? I want an education for my people that will elevate them. Why should we always be lying at the gate begging for bread, shelter, clothing, and jobs if we are free and educated? Do not get an education just to set it up as some useless symbolic monument to the black man in the Western Hemisphere. We need education that eliminates division among us. Acquire education that creates unity and makes us desire to be with our own.

We must begin at the cradle and teach our babies that they must do for self. They must not be like we, their fathers, who look to the slave-makers' and slave-masters' children for all. We must teach our children now with an enthusiasm exceeding that which our slave-masters used in having our forefathers imbed the seed of dependency within us.

We must educate ourselves and our children into the rich power of knowledge which has elevated every people who have sought and used it. We must give the benefit of our knowledge to the elevation of our people.

Critical Pedagogy

Who is going to teach you the knowledge of self? Who are you waiting for to teach you the knowledge of self? Surely, not your slave master, who blinded you to that knowledge of self. The slave master will not teach you the knowledge of self, as there would not be a master slave relationship any longer.

There is much misunderstanding among us because of our inferior knowledge of self. We have been to schools where they do not teach us the knowledge of self. We have been to the schools of our slave masters children. We have been to their schools and gone as far as they allowed us to go. That was not far enough for us to learn a knowledge of self. The lack of knowledge of self is one of our main handicaps. It blocks us throughout the world. If you were the world and you were a part of the world, you would also turn a man down if he did not know who he actually was.

To be rulers over rulers you have to have a superior wisdom, knowledge and understanding.

Critical Race Theory and Critical White Studies

We never had but one nation and one race. We didn't have race, as such, we had a nation. Race comes from the making of something from another.

Six thousand years ago, or to be more exact 6,600 years ago, as Allah taught me, our nation gave birth to another God whose name was Yakub. He started studying the life germ of man to try making a new creation(new man) whom our scientist foretold 8,400 years before the birth of Mr. Yakub, and the scientists were aware of his birth and work before he was born, as they are today of the intentions or ideas of the present world. (Note also has implications for genetics.)

When Yakub was six years old, one day, he was sitting down playing with two pieces of steel. He noticed the magnetic power in the steel attracting the other. He looked up at his uncle and said: "Uncle, when I get to be an old man, I am going to make a people who shall rule you." The uncle said: "What will you make; something to make mischief and cause bloodshed in the land." Yakub said: "Nevertheless, Uncle, I know that which you do not know."

What he really saw in playing with two pieces of steel was the magnetic power of attraction.

The one attracting and drawing the other under its power. In this, he saw an unalike human being, made to attract others, who could, with the knowledge of tricks and lies, rule the original black man-until that nation could produce one greater and capable of overcoming and making manifest his race of tricks and lies, with a nation of truth.

Teachings in the Social Sciences

History

We make such history once every 25,000 years. When such history is written, it is done by twenty-four scientists. One acts as Judge or God for the others and twenty three actually do the work of getting up the future nation, and all is put into one book and at intervals where such and such part or portion will come to pass, that people will be given that part of the book through one among that people from one of the Twelve (twelve major scientists) as it is then called a Scripture which actually means script of writing from something original or book.

There is significance of the number 24 Scientists and the 25,000 years. The number twenty-four Scientists used is in accordance with the hours in our day and the measurement of the circumference of our planet around the Equator and in the region of our Poles, Arctic, and Antarctic Oceans.

Economics

The economic plight of the black people of this land is so long been neglected by so-called leaders that even our own people have forgotten its basic importance. Our economic position remains at the bottom of the ladder because of this ineffective leadership and because so many of our people ignore the basic rules of a healthy economic life. We fail to develop self-leadership in economics.

I appeal to all Muslims, and to all the members of the original Black Nation in America, to sacrifice at least five cents from each day's pay to create an "Economic Savings Program" to help fight unemployment, abominable housing, hunger, and nakedness of the 22 million black people here in America who continue to face these problems.

We were brought here to work. We have worked! We are still workers. Some of us say, "What will we do if we do not work for the white man? How will we live?" I say, when you are free and independent you have a job! You have a tremendous task of doing something for self. You have the job of building a civilization for yourself as other free and independent people are doing for themselves.

Politics

It is difficult for me to advise my followers on taking part in the corrupt politics of our enemies, who are in complete control of the political affairs.

There are many black men and women who make splendid politicians. They could accomplish considerable good if they—like the white politician and his people—were given proper and equal recognition and justice for themselves and their people.

If our politicians are to serve us, they must have no fear of the white man when they plead our case in the white courts before white judges.

The Civil Rights Bill and integration will not stand and can never bring independence to you and your people, no matter who is President.

Anthropology

The black man is the first and last, maker and owner of the universe. From him came all brown, yellow, red and white people. By using a special method of birth control the black man was able to produce the white man.

Geography

The planet Earth, which is the home of Islam and is approximately twenty-five thousand miles in circumference. So the wise man of the East makes history or Koran to equal his home circumference—a year to every mile.

Teachings in the Sciences

There is no God who was here in the creation of the universe, but they produce gods from them and their wisdom lives in us.

Human beings are created according to the life of the universe (planets). Master Fard Muhammad, to whom praises are due forever, taught me that the original designer and maker of the universe created it on time and there is an end to it.

Scientists have learned by study that everything that we see and call universe is not endurable. It is gradually decaying.

The designer of the present universe made something that is absolutely unmatched and he made it out of the wisdom of man throughout the past until today.

This is like the creation of us. In the beginning, the God who created us had no material to use to begin his creation. He had only himself. Therefore out of darkness and the thoughtless and invisible he brought out the visible vision and thought and idea. He made a brain which had the power to cover the sphere of our thinking and to produce from that thought what image or vision that the brain cells could conceive.

The atom out of which man was created came from space. It was out in the space where he originated. An atom of life was in the darkness and he came out of that atom that was in space. Now you may wonder: how did that atom get in space? The history of space teaches us that at one time it was nothing but darkness. If there had been light for us to use our glasses on to, find if there was an atom of life in the darkness, before the atom exploded to show us what it was, we would tell you so. But we can't go that far.

Look at our creation from sperm to that of a human being. This is a marvelous piece of work of nature which bears witness to the first creation. We are making new creatures everyday. What helps to bring out about a new creation? When you make a new way of thinking in a person he is bound to do something new; for he cannot do something other than new since he has a new mind, new ideas. A new mind and new ideas produce a new thing.

Now he's making instruments to look at civilization on Mars. Well, when he see what's on Mars he won't see no mark of his. It's our Mars, our people, so God has taught me. He didn't know they were there until a few days ago. He use to look at Mars and just call it a star and that's all, but our fathers made it with intelligent beings like ourselves. They walk on two feet or hind. They are not animals. They are intelligent people. The marks that we see on Mars are not from ignorant, silly and uncivilized people. They show signs of civilization and they look similar to us, not exactly, but they look similar. They walk on two feet, and they're not white folks.

He made a Universe to always be improved upon; therefore, ever since the first sign of life in the Universe, it brought about other God's who were capable of adding to it all of the time.

Pluto or Plouton. Pluto is a scientific name representing 'A Little Fool.' It comes back to you and me. For 400 years we are off from our people, frozen-up in the power of the white man. We could not rotate according to the light and power of the wisdom of our Own God.

Pluto sits out there, something like four-billion, six-hundred-million miles from the Sun; but still just a touch of the Sun moves her.

Now they have also given us pictures of Mars, a planet that have life on it, they have been peeping in the window of Mars that life there looks near like us. Men growing seven and nine feet tall, and living a thousand of our earth years.[1]

Math

After learning Mathematics, which is Islam, and Islam is Mathematics, it stands true. You can prove it at no limit of time. Then you must learn to use it and secure some benefit while you are living, that is—luxury, money, good homes, friendship in all walks of life.

Religious Studies

The most important question of all questions that one could ask is, "Who is God?" It is like a child who does not know his father asking his mother to tell him the name of his father, wanting to know what his father looks like and if he favors his father. Can we not ask the same question who are seeking the knowledge of Our Father, God? Should we be called disbeliever's or infidels, just because we seek the truth or knowledge of Our Father, God? The mother may, in some cases, think it best to keep the name of her child a secret, as it was in the case of Mary and Joseph, 2,000 years ago. But, in the case of God, one would say that we all should know Him, but at the proper time.

Women's Studies

You and I may go to Harvard, we may go to York of England, or go to Al Ahzar in Cairo and get degrees from all of these great seats of learning. But we will never be recognized until we recognize our women.

She is your first nurse. She is your teacher. Your first lesson comes from your mother. If you don't protect your mother, how do you think you look in the eyes of other fellow human beings?

Automobiles

The people the new world will have a superior automobile and planes. They will not be fueled with the same fuel that they use today in this civilization. The fuel that they use contaminates the air.

Architecture

We are not only to build some temples, but we're out to build some towns and cities of our design, and not of the design of satan, who stole from us. We want to create a New Earth, a new us, and build a new world unalike Mr. Yakub's devil. We want to make a new world.

Architects are always in demand in a country where there's progress being made. You cannot build up a town or a city unless you have architects; you've got to have architects.

Banking

You have hundreds of millions of dollars laying in banks here in Chicago and other banks throughout America. You put your money in the white man's bank for him to use as he pleases. He gives you a little interest on it and you satisfied.

I propose establishing a black national bank for ourselves. You cannot see yourself trusting your own self. If you would give me a few of your million that you have lying in these banks—not a hundred million, just loan me ten million—I would show you one hundred million dollars for use of that ten million.

Agriculture

Let us capture the market of our people by producing their needs. We cannot produce our needs on soil of another.

What we must understand today is the importance of acquiring land of our own.

However you must go to the farms, till the earth, and produce your own food. Build stores and warehouses to preserve your food throughout season.

Raise cotton, corn, wheat, rye, rice, chicken, cattle, and sheep. The sheep would clothe us with its wool and feed us with its flesh. The cow would also serve as food for us, as well as hide being used in making shoes, belts, jackets, coats and hats.

Purchase real estate, buy farm and timberland. Convert the timber into lumber and build homes for yourselves as the white man is doing.

Islamic Studies

While teaching and representing a religion called "Islam" to you, the first important thing to do is answer the questions: What is Islam? Who is the author? Who are its prophets and people? Such questions could be answered in a few words or one could make books out of the answers. Briefly, "Islam" means the entire submission to the Will of Allah (God). It is, moreover, a significant name. Its primary significance is the making of peace, and the idea of "Peace" is the dominant idea in Islam.

Language

We must give the people a new language, you will find that in the Bible.

Health

Thousands of minor ailments disappear from us by eating the proper food and at the proper time—one meal a day. He (Allah) teaches us never to eat unless we are hungry. Eating when we are not hungry causes these minor ailments.

Aviation

We want airports. We want airplanes to go in and out of them.

Summary

Elijah Muhammad's teaching while primarily focused on the uplift and restoration of Black people in America had applications for every field of study. Perhaps the scholars who have openly tried to examine Elijah Muhammad's work have not been able to crack open the depth of what he taught because their areas of study have been limited to social sciences, particularly the study of history. Additionally, they have not been able to understand Elijah Muhammad's teaching because they have researched his work through the eyes of those who have purposefully tried to deceive the masses with regard to what he taught. Clearly Elijah Muhammad's teachings can be found in every field of study. The social sciences, the arts, the sciences, mathematics, business, technology, architecture, medicine, health and physical education were all a part of Muhammad's teaching. A careful examination of Muhammad's teaching will reveal that the modern research and technological advancement that we are currently experiencing is rooted in what Elijah Muhammad taught. The field of *Elijah Muhammad Studies* while rooted in the discipline of education is not limited to the dogma of teaching methods, school policy, or the technical mechanics of education. It is a deeper and more profound study situated in every discipline with the ultimate purpose of bringing forth the God essence in the human being. Thus it is a work that will require a new way of educating teachers. This will require a universal knowledge because the ultimate goal of Elijah Muhammad is to produce Gods.

Note

1. This coincides with pictures released by NASA. The video clearly depicts a Black man that is around seven to nine feet tall. For more information visit You Tube's website (Picture of a Man on Mars or Spooky Photo Proves Life On Mars.)

Postscript

The greatest work that we must do according to the mission, that almighty God in the person of Master Fard Muhammad give to me, it is to make known to the poor lost and found members of the Black nation, the true knowledge of self, their history, the knowledge of their slave master, and the nature of their slave master; and the creation of their slave master; and their nature; and their non birth record. By Elijah Muhammad

An Introduction to Elijah Muhammad Studies: The New Educational Paradigm has attempted to capture the mission of one of the most misunderstood personalities in American history. Elijah Muhammad an unlettered man born in rural Georgia, has been misunderstood by several of the writers who have attempted to examine his life's history. In the field of research, one of the more profound ways to understand what one is researching requires the researcher to go more deeply into the subject that is being researched. Those who have examined Elijah Muhammad have not tried to go into his mind so as to understand his thinking and the actual facts that form the basis of the body of knowledge that he brought. To really understand Elijah Muhammad and his mission, which was education, one has to work from an ethnographic research perspective. Creswell (1998) notes,

> As a process, ethnography involves a prolonged observation of the group, typically, through participant observation in which the researcher is immersed in the day to day lives of the people or through one on one interviews with members of the group. The researcher studies the meanings of behavior, language, and interactions of the culture sharing group. (p. 58)

The ethnographic research perspective allows the researcher to experience and live the reality of the individual or phenomena under study. By doing this the researcher is not guessing or assuming to theorize based on misjudged assumptions but the researcher has come to experience certain aspects of the phenomena under study. This powerful form of research will require one to walk in the shoes of the individual or group being researched. It is only when the researcher has come to understand in some profound way the essence of this experience are they able to articulate in a meaningful way the essence of this experience.

While some researchers have examined Elijah Muhammad, they have not been able to fully understand this man, because they have not been allowed to enter into his experience. If one were doing ethnographic research on homeless people, the value of this experience would require that the homeless people allow the researcher some acceptance into their culture. If the researcher is not allowed by the homeless people to interact and associate with them, then the researcher may not come to fully understand the life of a homeless person.

Therefore a sort of permission or acceptance by those being researched or examined is a prerequisite to fully understand the individual or phenomenon. As I reflect on many of the historical works of Elijah Muhammad, I find those with the most academic credibility to be in fact those most lacking in the deeper understanding of Elijah Muhammad. This has probably taken place because the researchers have been overwhelmingly as Woodson calls it mis-educated, to the point that they cannot really understand Elijah Muhammad. To really understand Elijah Muhammad one must look at more than just his life history but they must understand the relationship between what he taught, contemporary facts, and his educational experiences. Questions must be asked: Could a man with a fourth-grade education coming out of slavery disclose information that is more relevant today than it was 70 years ago? How could this unlettered man touch on every subject that is studied in major universities throughout the world? And finally how would we be able to get a glimpse into his mind?

Some might wonder if we would have to exhume the body of Elijah Muhammad to more fully understand this man and his mission. Fortunately, there is no body to exhume and the essence of Elijah Muhammad has ascended to another world only to return in a re and new form with a more profound body of knowledge than previously brought forth. This in itself is revolutionary as the basis for all of our studies is to come to a more profound understanding of how to conquer death. Examine it and think over it. All of our studies are supposedly leading us to a better life, one that will give us a more productive and longer life. But what happens when one has learned how to conquer death? What happens if one decides to experience death only to show forth their power to conquer death? Even more so what happens when death is experienced and conquered? What kind of education exists beyond the conquering of death? What kinds of ideas are produced in a world where death has been conquered? A greater understanding of these questions will help us to more fully understand this man Elijah Muhammad and the new educational paradigm. Perhaps in a world where death has been conquered we should expect it be filled with life. The ideas in that world will be filled with love, life, happiness, and unlimited progress. Elijah Muhammad throughout his teaching provides us with the educational basis for a New World. Muhammad's ultimate vision is a world where we will have transcended the impediments that keep us from fulfilling our purpose for existence.

Elijah Muhammad the revolutionary educator continues to impact people all over the world. I am reminded of his quote regarding the educational system of the aboriginal man, "The wisdom of the educational system of the aboriginal man of the earth has never been known to this world because the black man was put to sleep in order to let this world try itself at ruling. Now the rule of this world has been found to be dissatisfying and dissatisfaction is one hundred percent" (Muhammad, 1973, p. 93). This has caused me to reflect on the educational system that Elijah Muhammad envisioned. More importantly I think Elijah Muhammad was guiding us into thinking about an educational system that we would have to create using our mental capacities. Elijah Muhammad, unlike a regular classroom teacher, realized the importance of having his students engaged in the process of learning, so as to use their creative power to produce a new world. Muhammad never directly said what this new educational system would look like but this perhaps was a part of a strategy that would force us to think more deeply about the creation of an educational system that had never been witnessed. What does the educational system of the aboriginal man look like? Even deeper, what will that system look like when death is conquered? The new educational system is one that must be created, and according to Muhammad creation requires us to bring into existence that which does not exist. Muhammad taught that when God self-created himself in the darkness, he did not have a pattern or another that he could pattern his form after. It was through his ability to think through the darkness that he was able to create the self. This implies that we must use our creative thoughts to create an educational system that will go beyond the human plane. Our new educational system must move into the creation of Gods. This means that we can no longer view individuals as being useless but human beings should be regarded as having a God force within and a divine purpose for the manifestation of the wisdom of God. Farrakhan (2009) brilliantly explains the in-dwelling God force:

> But when you didn't have thought, before you could think, there was an intelligence working in you that is The Light of God and The Power of God. Even before the growth of intelligence, in the darkness we were being fashioned out of a tiny life germ—sperm mixed with ovum; and we were called into existence by what was in the head of that tiny sperm. And at the end of nine months, we came forth knowing nothing, but with the capacity to learn everything. (p. 31)

The curriculum put forth by Elijah Muhammad is the foundation for bringing forth new ideas which is in essence education.

Muhammad's curriculum started with the essential question: Who is God? This question and his response shocked the world. Muhammad started his educational program with pointing out that God is a man. More importantly Muhammad explained when God self created himself in the darkness the result was a Black man who was the original designer of the Universe. Muhammad talked about dark matter or dark energy out in the universe. In a recent finding regarding dark energy I was shocked to see how recent discoveries verify what Elijah Muhammad taught. The following is a recent article regarding dark energy, the universe, and man:

> These fluctuations were faint variations in temperature, and scientists have since followed up on those measurements to try to understand, for instance, dark matter—mass that no one has been able to see or measure but which must exist because of the amount of gravity measured in the universe.

> Some teams have come up with new theories of dark energy—a mysterious force that may be accelerating the expansion of the universe.

While the implications may far outlast humanity—the end of the universe may be coming in a few more billion years—Smoot has been clear on the need for the work. "It is extremely important for human beings to know their origins and their place in the world," Smoot said in a statement. (Fox, 2006)

The ideas and theories presented by the world's leading scientist can be understood more deeply by examining the work of Elijah Muhammad. Minister Farrakhan (2009) in a speech titled, *The Origin of Blackness* gives a more detailed explanation of this relationship between dark matter, the universe, and man, "Beyond the wall of the Universe there is darkness, and that darkness is not a shadow. That darkness is real. So when they talk about a "black hole," they are not talking about a shadow. They are talking about real darkness; and real darkness contains a Power" (p. 43). Tynnetta Muhammad (2006) adds, "Going back as early as six trillion years, according to the Divine Teachings of the Honorable Elijah Muhammad, the Blackness of the Original People corresponded to the material of darkness of the Universe in order for them to survive the intensity of the heat radiating from the light of the sun. Starlight was the original source of the material that makes up the human species and our DNA." Islam (2007) writes, "Indeed, the leading gods of the ancient Near East were not just black, but blue-black. This dark 'blueness' of the divine body had profound significance. It was not just any blue, but sapphire blue . . . This sapphiric heaven, called the 'sky-garment' of the gods, was associated with the divine body . . ." (p. 158).

As one compares the ideas of Elijah Muhammad with that of the best scholars in the world, one must ask, how could Elijah Muhammad an unlettered man have such profound knowledge? Elijah Muhammad's teachings form the basis for modern discovery, however, he has never been mentioned or referenced for having introduced the knowledge that has come to be a part of major research institutions in America. Elijah Muhammad's true teachings have not yet been disclosed to the masses. Additionally, his work prior to this writing has not been thoroughly examined as an educational endeavor that would shift the educational paradigm which forges the way for a New World.

In this small book, I have attempted to examine Elijah Muhammad's teachings as the basis for a paradigm shift that does not require temporal weapons, but one that requires "word power," which is light, energy, and ultimately life. This "word power" creates an internal revolution that can lead to an external revolution with the hope and possibility of creating a new world for all of humanity.

In conclusion, there were numerous books that have provided me with an academic theological understanding of Elijah Muhammad's mission. Elijah Muhammad's mission verifies the truth in the pronouncement given by Jesus to his disciples about the kingdom of heaven. Jesus, when questioned by his disciples about when the kingdom of God would come, replied the kingdom of God does not come with your careful observation because the kingdom of God is within you. Elijah Muhammad, prior to meeting his teacher Master Fard Muhammad, was like a seed that had been placed on a shelf. He did not bring forth any fruit. Once he met and was taught by Master Fard Muhammad, he was planted in a new soil and he began to produce new fruits. The impregnation of the word caused the kingdom of God to come forth from Elijah Muhammad's being, a kingdom that had been hidden or locked away. Elijah Muhammad was able to produce intellectual giants and revolutionary thinkers who have continued to impact the world.

Imagine what America and the world would be like if Malcolm X had never met Elijah Muhammad. Would Malcolm X have reverted back to his life of crime? What would he teach that would make him known throughout the world? What would have been the philosophical base for him to begin his quest for knowledge? How would Muhammad Ali be viewed if he had remained Cassius Clay? Would he have remained just an ordinary boxer who could have been killed in Vietnam? What would the world and America be like if there were no Louis Farrakhan? Would Farrakhan have remained Louis Walcott the calypso singer and entertainer? Would Farrakhan's name be mentioned as one of the people who impacted the world? What would have happened to the millions of people all across the world impacted by Elijah Muhammad's teachings? What would have become of the drug user who was transformed by Elijah Muhammad or the professor who was given a new idea that generated new research? What about the personal transformation and discipline that many incorporated into their daily lives?

Elijah Muhammad a man who completed only the fourth grade of school in his transition from rural Georgia to Detroit, Michigan, could never have imagined the enormous potential that lay dormant in him. The early years of his teaching and personal resurrection were initial steps in his growth into the knowledge of self. As he grew into greater understanding of self his ideas became more profound.

After reading about some of the students of Elijah Muhammad, I began to see that what many people saw as divisions that existed among his students were perhaps part of a process in producing a new world. Elijah Muhammad produced students who provided spiritual guidance to people from different persuasions. You can find from Elijah Muhammad a teacher who speaks the language of the Black nationalists, the multiculturalists, the Christian, the Buddhists, the rapper, the drug dealer, the scholar, the critical race theorists, the white studies proponents, the Latino, the Native American—the list could go on. The students produced by Elijah Muhammad speak in different tongues and are understood by people speaking in their own languages. For example some have noted contradictions between Imam Warith Deen Muhammad and his father Elijah Muhammad. However, one must consider that perhaps this was part of an ultimate plan that would attract people from diverse backgrounds. While each of the students might display a different coloring or perspective they have all ultimately been watered by the same water.

It is time now for reinterpretation of Elijah Muhammad. A new interpretation of Elijah Muhammad will move us into ideas about creating an entirely new world. A world where death has been conquered and humanity will be able to sing a new song, a song of life, a song of love.

References

Akbar, N. (1998). *Know thy self.* Tallahassee, FL: Mind Productions.

Anyon, J. (1981). Social class and the hidden curriculum of work. *Curriculum Inquiry* 11, No. 81: 27.

Apple, M. (2004). *Ideology and curriculum.* 3rd ed. New York: Routledge.

Asante, M. K. (2005). *Race, rhetoric, and identity: The architecton of soul.* Amherst, NY: Humanity Books.

Associated Press (1996, June 11). "Vinegar found in far away space."

Banks, J. (1973). *Teaching ethnic studies: Concepts and strategies.* Washington, DC: National Council for Social Studies.

———. (1996). *Multicultural education, transformative knowledge, and action: Historical and contemporary perspectives.* New York: Teachers College Press.

———. (2008). *An introduction to multicultural education.* 4th ed. Boston, MA: Pearson Education.

Bennett, C. (2003). *Comprehensive multicultural education*: Theory and practice. Boston, MA: Allyn and Bacon.

Berg, H. (2009). *Elijah Muhammad and Islam.* New York: New York University Press.

Chomsky, N. (2000). *Chomsky on mis-education.* Lanham, MD. Rowman and Littlefield.

Clegg, C. (1998). *An original man: The life and times of Elijah Muhammad.* New York: St. Martin's Griffin.

Creswell, J. (1998). *Qualitative inquiry and research design: Choosing among five traditions.* Thousand Oaks, CA: Sage Publications.

Curtis, E. (2002). *Islam in Black America: Identity, liberation and difference in African American Islamic thought.* Albany, NY: SUNY Press.

Doll, W. (1993). *A post-modern perspective on curriculum.* New York: Teachers College Press.

DuBois, W.E.B. (1982). *The souls of Black folk.* New York: Penguin Books.

Evanzz, K. (2001). *The messenger: The rise and fall of Elijah Muhammad.* New York: Random House.

Farrakhan, L. (1993). *Torchlight for America.* Chicago, IL: FCN Press.

———. (1996). *What a friend we have in Jesus.* Chicago, IL: Final Call Videotape.

———. (2005). *The purpose of knowledge.* Final Call Online Edition.

———. (2006). *Education is the key.* Chicago, IL: FCN Publishing.

———. (2008a). *The education challenge: A new educational paradigm for the 21st Century.* Chicago, IL: Final Call.

———. (2008b). *A new beginning.* Chicago, IL: Final Call.

Fox, M. (2006). *Space ripples discovery changed everything.* Reuters News.

Freire, P. (2000). *Pedagogy of the oppressed.* New York: Continuum.

Ghulan, M. (1996). *Muhammad: An Islamic perspective.* Lanham, MD: University Press of America.

Gollnick, D. & Chinn, P. (2006). *Multicultural education in a pluralistic society* 7th ed. Upper Saddle River, NJ: Prentice Hall.

Hakim, N. (1997a). *The theology of time* 3rd ed. Atlanta, GA: M.E.M.P.S. Publication.

————. (1997b). *The black stone: The true history of Elijah Muhammad: Messenger of Allah.* Atlanta, GA: M.E.M.P.S Publications.

————. (2002). *Yakub: The father of man-kind.* Atlanta, GA: M.E.M.P.S. Publication

Halasa, M. (1990). *Elijah Muhammad: Religious leader.* New York, Philadelphia: Chelsea House Publishers.

Handa, M. L. (1986) *Peace paradigm: Transcending liberal and Marxian paradigms.* Paper presented in International Symposium on Science, Technology and Development. New Delhi, India.

Hassan-El, K. (1999). *The Willie Lynch letter and the making of a slave.* Chicago: IL. Lushena Books.

Hilliard, A. (2001). Race, identity, hegemony, and education: What do we need to know now? In W. H. Watkins, J. Lewis, & V. Chou, *Race and education: The role of history and society in educating African American students,* (pp. 7-33). Needham Heights, MA: Allyn and Bacon.

Howard, G. (2006). *We can't teach what we don't know: White teachers in multiracial schools.* 2nd ed. New York: Teacher College Press.

Islam, T. (2007). *Master Fard Muhammad: Who is he? Who he is not?* Atlanta, GA: All in All Publishers.

————. (2007). *The truth of God.* Atlanta, GA: All in All Publishers.

Kincheloe, J. (2007). Foreword in McLaren, P., *Life in schools: An introduction to critical pedagogy in the foundations of education.* 5th ed. Boston, MA: Allyn and Bacon.

Kincheloe, J. & Steinberg, S. (1997). *Changing multiculturalism.* Buckingham, PA: Open University Press.

Kliebard, (1995). *The struggle for the American curriculum: 1893–1958.* New York: Routledge.

Kubow, P. & Fossum, P. (2006). *Comparative education: Exploring issue in international context.* 2nd ed. Upper Saddle River, NJ: Pearson.

Kuhn, T.S. (1962). *The structure of scientific revolutions.* Chicago: University of Chicago Press.

Ladson-Billings, G. (eds.) (2003). *Critical race theory perspectives on social studies: The profession, policies, and curriculum.* Greenwich, CT: Information Age Publishing.

Lincoln, E. (1994). *The Black Muslims in America.* 3rd ed. Trenton, NJ: Africa World Press.

Lloyd, G. (1998). Spinoza and the education of imagination. In Amelie Rorty, *Philosophers on education: new historical perspectives,* (pp. 157-72). New York: Routledge.

Lomax, L. (1962). *When the word is given.* Cleveland, OH: World Publishing Company.

Macedo, D. (2000). Introduction in N. Chomsky, *Chomsky on miseducation.* Lanham, MD. Rowman and Littlefield Publishers.

Marable, M. (2007). *The Malcolm X project at Columbia University.* (Retrieved from: http://www.columbia.edu/cu/ccbh/mxp/mxstun.html)

Marsh, C. & Willis, G. (2003). *Curriculum: Alternative approaches, ongoing issues.* 3rd ed. Upper Saddle River, NJ: Prentice-Hall.

McLaren, P. (2007). *Life in schools: An introduction to critical pedagogy in the foundations of education.* 5th ed. Boston, MA: Allyn and Bacon.

Morris, V. (1968). An overview of: Existentialism and education. In Joel Park, *Selected readings in the philosophy of education,* (pp. 303-15). New York: MacMillan Company.

Muhammad, C. (2005). *Ideas on education: True education leads to a full and complete freedom.* Chicago, IL: Instant Publishers.

Muhammad, D. (2000). Scholar C. Eric Lincoln dies at 75. Retrieved from: http://www.finalcall.com/national/c_eric_lincoln5–30–2000.htm.

Muhammad, E. (1965). *Message to the Blackman in America.* Chicago, IL: Final Call.

———. (1973). *The fall of America.* Newport News, VA: National Newport News and Commentator.

———. (1974). *Our savior has arrived.* Chicago, IL: Final Call.

———. (1993). *History of the Nation of Islam.* Atlanta, GA: Secretarius MEMPS Publication.

Muhammad, J. (1996). *This is the one: The most honored Elijah Muhammad, We need not look for another.* 3rd ed. Phoenix, AZ: Book Company.

Muhammad, J. & L. Farrakhan (2006). *Closing the Gap.* Chicago, IL: FCN Publishing.

Muhammad, N. (October 7, 2008). *How to educate black boys. Black caucus workshop examines tough issues.* Chicago, IL: Final Call.

Muhammad, T. (2001). *Understanding time-past, present and future being perfect.* Final Call Online Edition.

———. (2006). *The proper meaning of Blackness and its relation to our visit to the Tomb of King Pacal in Palenque, Chiapas.* Chicago, IL: Final Call.com News.

Nieto, S. & Bode, P. (2008). *Affirming diversity: The socio-political context of multicultural education.* 5th ed. New York: Longman.

Noah, J. & Eckstein, M.A. (1998). *Doing comparative education: Three decades of collaboration.* Hong Kong: Comparative Education Research Centre.

Noel, J. (2008). *Notable selections in multicultural education.* 2nd ed. New York: McGraw Hill.

Oakes, J. (1985). *Keeping track: How schools structure inequality.* New Haven, CT: Yale University Press.

Okafor, V. (2006). *Towards an understanding of Africology.* Dubuque, IA: Kendall Hunt Publishing Company.

Ozmon, H. and Craver, S. (2008). *Philosophical foundations of education,* 8th ed. Upper Saddle River, NJ: Pearson Prentice Hall.

Parker, W. (2001). *Social studies in elementary education.* Upper Saddle River, NJ: Prentice Hall.

Pinar, W. (2004). *What is curriculum theory?* Mahwah, NJ: Lawrence Erlbaum Associates.

Pinar, W., Reynolds, W., Slattery, P., & Tubman, P. (2008). *Understanding curriculum.* New York: Peter Lang.

Pipes, D. (2000). *How Elijah Muhammad Won.* Retrieved from website: www.danielpipes.org/article/341.

Pitre, A. (2008). *The educational philosophy of Elijah Muhammad. Education for a new world.* 2nd ed. Lanham, MD: University Press of America.

Pitre, A., Ray, R., and Pitre, E. (2008). *The struggle for black history: Foundations for a critical black pedagogy in education.* Lanham, MD: University Press of America.

Rassoull, A. (1992). *The theology of time.* Charlotte, NC: Conquering Books.

Shor, I. & Freire, P. (1987). *A pedagogy for liberation. Dialogues on transforming education.* Westport, CT: Bergin and Garvey.

Shujaa, M. J. (Ed.). (1994). *Too much schooling, too little education: A paradox of Black life in White societies.* Trenton, NJ: Africa World Press.

Slattery, P. (2006). *Curriculum development in the postmodern era,* 2nd ed. New York: Routledge.

Spivey, D. (2003). *Fire from the soul. A history of the African American struggle.* Durham, NC: Carolina Academic Press.

Spring, J. (2006). *American education.* New York: McGraw Hill.

Spring, J. (2007). *Deculturalization and the struggle for equality: A brief history of the education of dominated cultures in the United States.* New York: McGraw Hill.

Watkins, W. (2001a). *The White architects of Black education: Ideology and power in America 1865-1954.* New York: Teachers College Press.

————. (2001b). Blacks and the curriculum: From accommodation to contestation and beyond. In Watkins, W., Lewis, J. & Chou, V. *Race and education: The roles of history and society in educating African American students,* (pp. 40-66). Needham Heights, MA: Allyn and Bacon.

Woodson, C. G. (1999). *The mis-education of the Negro.* 11th ed. Trenton, NJ: First Africa World Press.

Yunus, M. (2007). *Creating a world without poverty: Social business and the future of capitalism.* New York: Public Affairs.

Index